THE UNSPOKEN TRUTH

a memoir

LISA ZARCONE

ISBN: 978-1-5356-0148-1

Dedication

John and Joann Sega and my beautiful brother, John Patrick…

My special family; without them this story could never have been told,
As if we were not together in the beginning, it would never have been…

Love you three with all my heart and soul, we are endlessly bound together By our love, courage and strength… We have all traveled down difficult and unique Roads; with our paths intertwined forever.

I feel your love and encouragement every day of my life,
and I am grateful for All the gifts your love has given me throughout the years!

I am truly blessed.

Note to the Reader

When I decided to write this book, I wanted it to be viewed through MY eyes, as a child.

Please remember while you are reading, my expressions and thoughts are through a six-year-old's eyes. Some of my thoughts may seem odd or out of place, but a child's mind sees things quite differently than an adult!

This was challenging for me, as I had to tap into my thoughts and emotions from my memory as a kid.

For example, try to think back to your earliest childhood memory. Once you have one in mind, try to remember the weather that day, or the time of year. What are you feeling in this moment? Try to remember the feelings attached to this memory—good or bad or sad or happy. Does it seem animated to you?

When you draw from the emotions of your inner child, it opens you up to a whole NEW world of your internal thoughts. Once we are grown, most of us tuck that creative and vulnerable way of thinking aside and replace it with logical and responsible thoughts and feelings.

I really tried to express this throughout my story so you can understand how I was feeling in the moment, and how my thought process changed as I got older. I also repeat myself at times, and that is another way children process, through repetition of thought and doing.

Now here we go. Are you ready for an emotional ride?

I hope you as the reader get as much out of my story as I did when I wrote it!

Contents

Prologue

Deep in Thought

At Palm Beach International Airport early in the afternoon I am boarding a plane to go back home. As I stand there in line I look around at my surroundings—people are coming and going. The hustle and bustle of this busy world we live in encompasses me like a bubble of loud confusion. At the moment I feel so small, so insignificant to all around me. My eyes are glassy, and my face is pale and sullen. One small tear drips from my eye as I stand there waiting.

"Ticket please," I hear echoing from so far away.

I am instantly snapped back into reality. "Yes, here is my ticket," I say with a stutter.

The attendant looks at me, eyeing me intently, and asks, "Are you all right, miss?"

I say, "Yes, I am," and I quickly board the plane.

As I take my seat I am oblivious to everything around me. I sit by the window as always, and my mind begins to wander. I am thinking that I have traveled home like this countless times before. I would always be so excited to see my family, and thought about how much I missed them while I was gone. I also thought about what was going on with them during my absence, and how they all survived without me. My family is vibrant and full of energy, so I could only imagine the stories that would be told when I finally arrived home. The best part of my homecoming will always be, getting off the plane and seeing my handsome husband standing there waiting for me with his brilliant smile and warm brown eyes. I look forward every time to that moment when we embrace. He hugs me and tells me he loved me. He always makes me feel safe and complete.

Coming home this time is quite different. This time, with a heavy heart, I have to say good-bye to my father, this strong, powerful presence of a man. My dad, my phone buddy, as I call him. He was just a phone call away—in times of joy or sorrow, or just to say hey what is going on at your end of the world. My dad passed away after a long, hard battle with heart disease and diabetes. He was only 69, and had so much more he wanted to do in this life. I had sat with him as he passed, talking to him telling him how much I loved him and to look for my brother. Dad, "When you see Jon Jon, go be at peace, no more pain, no more sorrow." At that moment, he opened his eyes and looked up into the corner of the room, and I knew right there and then my brother had arrived to take him home. I could feel his presence so warm and powerful. "Candle in the Wind" was playing on the radio at the moment of his death followed by "Lean on Me," and just like that, he was gone.

"Cloudy out today, isn't it? I hope we do not get turbulence."

Once again I am shaken back into reality. I look over at a little old woman, so small and frail, wearing a pink sweater, sitting next to me. I try to smile and say, "Yes, it is cloudy for sure, but we will be fine. No worries", and I touch her hand to give her reassurance. Even in my time of great sorrow, I still felt the need to give compassion to others. It is in my nature to do so; I was blessed with this gift. It felt like my dad put this woman next to me to show me that life does go on, and there is still so much more work to do.

I then turn away and pick up the ring that once draped over my father's ring finger now hanging on my necklace. With tear-filled eyes, I pull the ring close to my lips. My hands are shaking as I rub his ring over my lips, giving it a kiss. I then close my eyes and begin to think back to a time when I was a child. The moment in my life that changed everything.

THE BEGINNING....

LOSING MY BROTHER,
LOSING MY FAMILY.

CHAPTER 1

Tragedy through the Eyes of a Child

Chapter 1

Tragedy through the Eyes of a Child

Here I am six years old sitting on a chair in Grandma Theresa's kitchen. I am a petite little girl with long brown hair and big blue eyes. My striped shirt is pink, brown, and orange, with my pleated pants of brown to match. It is 1972, and the style of clothing was quite unique and bold! I am listening to the silence. The only sound is the clock ticking loudly on the wall. As I stare at the minute hand moving along I am counting each click in my head as I sway my ponytails back and forth in an uneasy rhythm. I feel the need to move, but something inside me tells me to sit still. I am in the company of my grandparents, and we are just sitting there staring at each other. I am studying them in my mind as my grandfather is twittering his fingers on the kitchen table, thump thump, thump thump! My grandmother is silently praying as I am watching her lips move but not a sound is coming out of her mouth. Thump, thump, thump, click, click, click! I am going back and forth between the two sounds, as I sway my ponytails to the eerie beat.

My grandmother is a slender woman with a pointy nose, and at first appearance you would think she is tall. It is actually her hair that is tall, as she had it teased up to perfection in the bubble hairstyle that was in during the 70s. Normally, she is moving all over the place with such high energy directing my grandfather to help her in the kitchen, which he happily does on a normal day. My grandfather is just the opposite. He is a short man, balding and round. He is a true Italian. He usually has the sweetest smile on his face that was so comforting and inviting. He chuckled when he spoke. His voice is always filled with laughter, but not on that day.

Seeing them like this really starts to bother me. I wonder why weren't they talking? They look like statues. It scares me to see them sitting there like this. My grandparents are usually loud, and talking all the time. I feel so uncomfortable. I don't know what to do with myself, so I just keep on counting the clicks of the clock, and the beats of my grandfather's fingers. As I continue to look around the room, the sun is beaming in through the windows. My grandmother's ruffled curtains are perfectly pinned back, with the ruffles swaying back and forth from the heater below. She always kept her home in perfect order, and her curtains and drapes throughout the home never had a wrinkle. Her kitchen was usually warm and enticing with many wonderful smells of her cooking. There was always a fresh pot of sauce on the stove as well as other endless pots boiling and simmering; but on this day nothing was brewing but the calm before the storm.

It is eerily silent. I feel like something is not right. For some reason, I have a sick feeling in my little belly. I am uneasy not knowing what I should do so I continue wiggling in my chair waiting for something to happen, but not knowing what that something was. The silence is finally broken when we hear footsteps in the back hall, and the old wooden floorboards creak loudly. My grandmother jumps up in a nervous twitch, and rises to her feet instantly. My grandfather sits still leaning forward waiting to see who was coming through the door. The back door suddenly opens with a cold breeze, which flies right across my face. I watch anxiously as the handle turns slowly and I see my dad's hand first.

My father and mother enter through the door and are now standing before us in the kitchen.

I look up at my parents, and my dad has tears in his eyes; he looks worn out and broken. This big man who is usually so strong with an era of greatness around him looks like a lost puppy that was just tossed out into the cold. I then immediately shift my attention to my mom trying to examine the scene as quickly as I could. I feel so anxious and out of place. My little heart is racing right out of my chest. When I make eye contact with her she looks blank and dead inside. Her eyes look black and cold as she stares past me. I realize in an instant that my mom is once again gone. I am terrified at this sight before me.

As a small child I remember brief moments when my mom was my mom, and then in the blink of an eye she would be gone. It is amazing at this young age I understood this process my mom would go through. I was very aware of her emotional instabilities. I was drawn to it because it made me feel on edge all the time. I never felt comfort from her, only anxiousness. I would watch her all the time, and examine her. I remember thinking, what is going to happen next? Who will she switch into now? Is this a game she is playing? Is my mom lost in there, trying to get out? What do I do if she never comes back? Who will take care of me? These are all the thoughts that would go through my head continually. As I am looking at her so intently, I can still see her face on that dreadful day. I can envision myself sitting there just staring at her. This moment is etched into my memory forever. It is haunting.

Then, my dad kneels down in front of me, and simply says, "Lisa, your brother is gone. He went to heaven with the angels." Then he puts his head in my lap and sobs like a baby. I put my hand on his head and just watch him cry. I stroke his hair as ke keeps saying, "My son is gone. My son is gone! What am I going to do?" I remember looking around the room at the faces of my family, and feeling their sorrow. My grandfather was standing there openly sobbing shaking his head and covering his face. His cries were so loud and daunting. My grandmother can't take it another moment and runs out into the other room, where she is hysterical, and totally inconsolable. She is screaming at the top of her lungs, NO, NO, NO, over and over again like an unchaining melody of heartbreaking sorrow. The weeping and screaming in this twisted harmony of death was deafening, and I was in panic mode, but I was frozen in fear at the same time.

With this entire scene happening before my eyes, what really stands out to me besides the loud cries of my family, was my mom. She was robotic, standing there with her eyes black and cold. The shock was obviously too much for her to handle and she seemed to go on autopilot. She starts to shake and she mumbles something to herself. I cannot understand what she is saying. I am watching her mouth move wildly out of control but nothing is really coming out. She never makes eye contact with me, and I do not even think she ever saw me sitting there. I then watch in horror as she leans back on the wall, sliding down it slowly, dropping to the floor. As she is sitting motionless, which it seems she will for an eternity, I turn my focus back to my dad. I don't know what to do so I continue to stroke my dad's hair and whisper in his ear, "Its ok, Daddy. You still have me."

I am six years old trying to grasp this whole thing. My brother just died of Leukemia, my family is going crazy, and I feel invisible. Everything is out of control, and there is nothing I can do but sit and feel helpless. I am so scared I just want to cry. I am looking down at my little Keds sneakers with the white rubber tips that are on my feet.

As I kick my feet back and forth, I continue to hold on to my daddy so tight, never wanting to let go. In this moment I felt like if I stopped holding him, I would lose him forever. My thoughts go back to my brother, *is he really gone?*

It was just a few weeks ago that he tried out for little league baseball. He was not feeling well that day, I do remember that, but he insisted on going to try out. He loved to play ball. My dad tried to talk him out of going, but he insisted that he needed to do it. I also remember the phone call that came in just a few days later, when the coach told my dad that my brother did NOT make the team. The disappointment in his eyes stayed with me. This was another moment when I was standing there besides him, as my dad explained why he didn't make the team. My brother just put his head down and walked slowly to his room saying, "It's ok, Daddy. Next year, right?"

The following day my brother woke up with a fever and spots all over him. He had the chicken pox. He was very, very sick. My parents tried to keep me away from him, but that was impossible. As he was lying on the couch crying in pain, I would run to his side to try to comfort him. It was horrible to see him so uncomfortable. Every day just seemed to be worse than the day before. The last few days of his illness, my parents sent me to stay with my grandparents, as it was too much for my mom to handle. I did not want to go, and I remember crying and begging my mom to let me stay. She refused to listen to me, and just said, "Go, Lisa!" My grandmother tugged at me to make my way to the door, but I needed to talk to my brother before I had to go, and I started to panic. I pulled away from her and ran over to him. I got as close as I could to him, holding onto his arm. He rolled over to see what all the fuss was about. He was pale, with spots all over his face. He managed to give me a half smile.

I kissed him on the forehead, and I said to him, "Please get better so we can go outside and play. I miss you and I love you!" He looked at me with half-closed eyes and weakly said, "I love you, too." These were the last words that we spoke to one another.

THAT WOULD BE THE LAST TIME THAT I SAW HIM ALIVE...

My brother, John Patrick Sega, born on March 17, 1963, was nine years old and full of life, and in a blink of an eye he was gone. He was a big boy for his age, husky in size with thick, dark brown hair and chocolate eyes that would melt anyone's heart. He was this kind, gentle giant who loved sports and his family. He was an incredibly strong young man with a lot of fight inside of his soul. He was my entertainer, as he always made me laugh. He was my hero! He lost his battle against this horrible disease that he fought gallantly for almost two years.

The pain he endured with all the treatments were horrible. He did this just so he could live. He did not want to be apart from his family, he told me that on several occasions. He would cry sometimes and I would talk to him. He was my best friend. I looked up to him, and he was so loving and kind to me. We were young but very close. We were definitely kindred spirits. We never fought, and we both had a great love of animals and nature. We would play in the yard, and run through the neighborhood, pretending we were on great adventures together. We were unstoppable!

The last year of his life brought us even closer together, as I would be by his side during all of his treatments. We would talk about everything; we would even talk about life and death. He did not want to die. He told me he was scared. I would say to him, it's ok you are not going anywhere! I did not want him to be scared, that made me so upset and angry. I wanted to protect him, just as much as he protected me. I would think to myself all the time, why would he have to leave me, or our family?

It is really sinking in now, as I am looking and listening to everyone openly sob. I felt like I was floating almost dream-like, as the sounds of my family sobbing seem to get louder and more animated. My head starts spinning, and I feel like I am going to throw up or pass out. I am sure the shock of it all was now hitting me, as I am trying to process the words. He is gone! He is gone! I do not think I got it. I am now getting all these flashes of moments with my brother before my eyes, as my head continues to spin. I can feel him, and I want to reach out to him, but he is not there. I feel so lightheaded but heavy at the same time.

My lip starts to quiver, and my eyes well up. My little body is shaking as I try to hold back the tears. I am afraid to cry, I am afraid to move, I am afraid to breathe, so I just sit and shake. As my thoughts wandered I was brought to a past memory of he and I outside on the deck getting ready to eat lunch together on a warm summer day.

ALWAYS THE TEACHER...

It was a hot summer day, and my mom called us in for lunch. We are in our bathing suits as we had been running through the sprinklers together. The sun was bright and hot, and the cool water on our skin felt wonderful. We were pretending that we were swimming in the ocean with the dolphins kicking and jumping up and down. We had the best imaginations that took us everywhere!

My mom calls us again, so we stop playing and come running. We were laughing and chatting about how we are going to go back to the ocean after lunch, as we were coming up on the deck. My mom had our lunches placed out perfectly for us, with our red Kool-Aid in paper cups. Red Kool-Aid was my favorite, so I was excited. As we approached the table she was nowhere to be found. We sat down, and I looked over through the screen door, and there she is, our mother, sitting on the couch smoking her cigarette in silence as she mutters to herself puffing away and crying. I am perplexed.

My brother said to me, "Lisa don't worry about mommy she will be ok, let's just eat lunch, and get back to our game." As we eat, I cannot help but stare at her, and my brother starts making faces at me, and wiggling in his chair, sticking out his tongue to make me laugh. I giggled. He always had a way to distract me from the sadness in our home. As we laughed together I finished my Kool-Aid and wanted more. My brother said to me, "Lisa don't ask her, just eat." I couldn't help myself I was thirsty. It was a hot day, and I wanted more! Again, he said, "Don't ask please, I'm telling you, you need to listen to me!!" but I did not listen to him, and I asked the question anyways! He was glaring at me!

I yelled into the house, Mom, "I want more Kool-Aid, I am dying of thirst out here!" As I waited impatiently NOTHING happened. I looked at him and he was shaking his head feverishly, but again I asked, as I was a persistent little girl. "Mom, Mom where is my kool-aid, I am thirsty!" You would think this would be a simple request right? Well, all of a sudden she came bursting out of the door, with this evil look in her eyes, yelling at me with the container in her hand, waving it about. Red Kool-Aid splashed all over the deck. As I looked at her in horror, she pored the Kool-Aid and it spilled everywhere because as she was poring it she was screaming at me. "You brat, you always want something, why can't you be good like your brother!" I started to cry, and she continued to banter at me for being a crybaby, then she walked back into the house slamming the screen door behind her. With tear-filled eyes I look up, there was red juice all over the table, and as I looked to my brother for comfort he said to me, "See I told you, do not ask her! You need to listen to me, I know better!" He knew all too well of her behaviors, and the biggest clue was when she would sit and cry, mumbling to herself, stay clear! Lesson learned!

Who is going to teach me now, that he is gone? Who is going to protect me from these awful moments when my mom is not my mom? That is what popped into my head when I was thinking of this particular moment…

The continued sobbing snaps me back into reality…

So I look back down at my dad who is now looking to me for comfort, still repeating the same words over and over again. He is gone! He is gone! This big man, my DAD, sprawled out on the floor with his head still in my lap weeping like a baby. I do not know what to think! With all the adults in the room, he was looking to me for support even back then. I am lost for words!

Anyways, what words could a kid come up with to even help the situation? How am I supposed to comfort my dad, when I do not truly understand what is going on? The room continues to spin. The only way to describe it is like I was tossed into a vortex spinning out of control and then dropped into a world that is foreign and strange! The mind of a child sees things so differently, so animated and bazaar.

I look to my right and my mom is still sitting on the floor talking a mile a minute to her-self, but I could not understand a word she was saying. It was like she was speaking another language altogether. I look straight ahead and my grandfather stands right in front of me face buried in his hands crying softly, and I could still hear the screams of my grandmother coming from the other room.

The sadness so overwhelming, I cry out silently to my brother, saying, "What do I do now? Help me, help me, please come save me now and make this all go away! Please make this nightmare go away." I am desperate for help. I close my eyes tight, faced wrinkled, tears streaming down, and I wait a moment. When I open my eyes and nothing has changed, I am devastated!

I guess that is when it all started. That is when this six-year-old little girl began being the caretaker of others. My family is now coming to me looking for support. Here it is right in my lap, this moment in time that will change my life forever. It is amazing how one single moment changes a life path.

TRAGEDY THROUGH THE EYES OF A CHILD

A sick child is all I hear, "my god it is a parent's worst fear." I watch, I listen, I tag along, nobody to shelter me from the storm... The storm of reality about to hit, I am losing my brother, I am only six... Nobody seems to notice me there, lost in the shuffle of my fading family in despair...

One day he is here, next day he is gone, how confused am I, with no one to lean on... I sit in a chair wide eyes looking around, seeing my mother fall to the ground. The sobs of my grandparents echo in my head, all I hear is "He is dead, He is dead..." Now my dad stands over me, he says, I am sorry he is gone, how are we to be? Now a family of only three...

Never allowed to say good-bye, here today, now he has to fly, soar to the heavens up above, an angel he is, maybe a dove...

Time goes by this child so confused, I stand on my lawn look up At the sky, "Where are you, my brother?" I begin to cry, you left me alone in this big scary world, how do I survive, which way do I turn? I trip; I fumble my way through life, waiting for guidance, while I pray every night... Then a dream comes to me as I sleep, my brother tells me he is the one in my back seat. In the rearview mirror as I drive, I see a face, his eyes twinkle so bright. He speaks to me through my mind, "Little sis, I never left you, I am right by your side..."

CHAPTER 2
Alone I Weep

Chapter 2

Alone I Weep

I AM SIX YEARS OLD. I was just told my brother died and went to heaven.

Did I really get it? There was so much chaos exploding around me, and I was taking it all in. Everywhere I turned something was happening. Family and friends were coming in the back door and consoling my parents. There were people everywhere, talking and crying. Then the front doorbell rings! My aunt runs to open the front door, and this strange man, a doctor, comes rushing in. He attends to my grandmother immediately, and gives her a sedative. I hear him mutter a few words to my grandfather. My grandfather thanks him, and just as quickly as he came he was gone. I am so confused and wonder why this doctor came to our house? Is my grandmother sick? Is she going to end up in that horrible hospital like my brother? After all he did give her a needle, just like my brother had so many times before. I watched my brother get needles in his back all the time, as part of his treatments.

I start to feel anxious, and I panick. I don't know what to do, and nobody was paying attention to me. My family doesn't even realize I was watching the whole thing. I crawled under the dining room table, and begin to rock. I peek out between the chairs and I see my grandmother who is now lying in bed weeping until she finally falls asleep. When I finally feel strong enough, I come out from under the table and walk by her room to check on her. I do this several times, even going in to watch her breath. I want to make sure she is still alive and not in heaven with my brother. I feel almost invisible as I stand there just watching her breath. My feet on the other hand feel heavy like lead weights pulling me down to the point where I cannot move. My aunt happens to walk by the room and sees me staring at my grandmother. She looks angry and points for me to come out. I slowly move out of the room and as our eyes meet I am frightened. She says to me, "Go find something to do and leave everyone alone!" I scurry off like a little field mouse running for cover.

People continue to come and go, and my parents are crying. I feel so alone. So, so alone! Nobody is thinking about me, and what I am feeling and thinking about? What I was thinking at that time was that I am floating around like a little butterfly, flickering from one room to the next silently. Moving through the air guided by the wind, and nobody sees me. Invisible to all, as I flutter endlessly trying to get the attention of somebody, anybody! Have you ever been outside and this little butterfly comes up to you fluttering frantically, and you swat it away. Then it continues to come back until you take notice? That is exactly how I felt, but nobody paid attention to me, and I continued to flutter hoping someone would eventually take notice.

I am also thinking, what just happened? Is my brother coming home later?

Why did they leave him at that horrible hospital? That nasty place where they would take me to watch him get stuck in his back with several needles! I would have to sit there and endure watching his treatments and see him cry out in pain. The place where they would draw purple lines on him and put him under bright lights that would later make him sick. A place where the morgue was right next to where he would get radiation treatments, and I would watch them wheel dead people into the tunnel. When I think of that place and the horrible memories attached to it, I feel sick inside.

At times I would see the dead people sit up on the gurney and they would wave to me. It puzzled me, but I would wave back, as they went by. I felt bad for them, as they too looked almost invisible as they popped through the white sheet. I could feel their sorrow and pain. I also felt connected to them, as I felt invisible too. Was this the mind of an imaginative child dealing with stress or, was I really seeing dead people as they were leaving. As they would wave goodbye to me, some were smiling and some were crying. Some of them were a little frightening, but I always sat still and just observed. They say children can see the dead. I believe that to be true, because as a child I saw the dead.

The next couple of days are a blur for me. I never was allowed to go to the wake or the funeral to say goodbye. I stayed with neighbors and even slept there until it was over. I do remember going back to my grandmother's house after the funeral. There were a ton of people their talking, eating, smoking, and crying. I was once again invisible to all wandering around the room taking it all in still completely confused. It was crazy to think that not even one person ever thought to discuss with me anything about my brother and where he had gone. All I remember is the words of my father, "Your brother had died and is now in heaven." That's it!!!! This is all I get, no other explanation. Even as a child, I remember feeling angry. I was angry with everyone, and not understanding why?

I wanted to talk, but I never had my moment so I remained silent in my many thoughts. Words were swirling around in my little head, and the thoughts were so profound beyond my years. I am so afraid for my brother, and worried that he was scared as he always was. He was in the dark now, a place that truly terrified him? I was thinking about how would I be able to protect him, if nobody tells me where to find him. I was also wondering when he was coming back from heaven so we could play. All these thoughts were rummaging through my head over and over again, and then what seemed like a minute the day was over. We pack up the car and go back home to our house where all his things are. I have not been home in days. As we pull up to the house, I am excited. All I could think of was that he must be there! It was the only logical conclusion that I could come up with that made sense to me. I jumped out of the car and run into the house as fast as I could to look for him. I was yelling, "Jon Jon, where are you? Where are you?" I went through the door, and he was not there. I ran into his room expecting to see him sitting there playing with his matchbox cars that he loved so much but nothing! It was empty and all of his things were just how he had left them, before he went to the hospital. I looked around and felt that the most important thing was missing—Jon Jon. This is the room that I would sneak in at night to climb in bed with him, because he was so scared. He would cry at night, and I would go comfort him. He would call me from down the hall. He said there were things in his room floating around they frightened him. At that time I began to see them too. I was scared, but I wanted to protect him. How unusual, me the little sister wanting to protect my big brother from his fears.

Out of mouths of babes..

Lisa are you awake? I hear his voice from down the hall. Yes, Jon Jon I am What is wrong? I am scared again come see me. Ok, I am coming. I climb out of bed and run down the hall as fast as I can because I am scared of the dark. I jump into his bed and we lay there looking up at the ceiling. I ask, what are you afraid of? I am afraid of dying, he says to me still looking up at the ceiling. I rub my hand on his face and say, please don't go; I want you to stay with me forever! I will stay with you Lisa forever I promise. Will you really die, Jon? Yes, he says the angels told me I would be going soon. Tell them I said they couldn't take you away from me! They said I have no choice, but I can come back and visit any time. OK, so if you go it will be just for a little bit then you can visit any time you want? He says yes any time. Then I will be waiting for you, and maybe one day I can go with you and the angels will teach me how to fly. He laughed at me, and then we laughed together. I love you so much Lisa. I love you too, Jon Jon…

What were we seeing back then?

I was told later on that our home was built on an Indian burial ground and village. I did do research and that is the case. They were the Quinnapiac Indians. They farmed and were fishermen, as we lived between a lake and the ocean. The tribe was almost totally wiped out by the plague, and the remaining few went north and joined another tribe. So, were we seeing spirits? Our home was never comfortable, and as children we were scared. After my brother passed away, my home got even scarier, for many reasons, which I will touch upon another time. I do believe it was haunted. I would see people standing in the corner of my room just staring at me. There was an Indian Chief that would come over and over again, standing there next to my bed holding some type of long stick with feathers on it. He would wave it at me, and I was terrified! I would also hear bangs on my wall that was connected to the basement, a place I detested, because it felt like all eyes were upon me, and I felt evil spirits were down there waiting to pounce.

MOMENT OF THE INDIAN…

I feel the need to add this in at this specific spot. When my brother would go for his treatments at Yale New Haven Hospital, I was always with him. My mother would always take me out of school on those days, and we would go there as a family, the four of us.

On one particular day I was sitting in the corner in a little chair. My brother was on the table, and the nurses came in to give him a treatment, which consisted of putting several needles in his lower back. (I know I have repeated myself a few times but this is how profound these memories are.) It was awful to watch him endure such pain, and his cries were deafening at times. So, as I am sitting there in this small red chair (I remember the color) I was looking around the room at anything that would take me away from what was actually happening.

I noticed there was a chalkboard on the side of the wall, and the picture on it was taunting me, calling out to me so to speak. It was an Indian Chief that someone had taken the time to draw. It was quite detailed, and had intricate lines on his chiseled face. To this day, I can still see that image of him, staring at me, his eyes speaking without his mouth moving.

I am now focused only on him! The room was filled with nurses and doctors, my parents and me. There is a lot of movement and commotion. The room is white and sterile, not inviting at all, but with everything happening around me, all I can see and hear is this Indian.

I am compelled to get up from my chair and walk over to the board, as I am staring at him so intently nobody seems to take notice. I am mad as I look into his eyes, and I pick up the eraser and erase him. I remember how hard I was pressing down on the board going back and forth faster and faster until he was totally gone. Then I just stood there staring at the blank board. My thoughts…I am six years old and all I could think of was making him go away!!!

Then I picked up the chalk and started to draw my own version of this Indian, but not the one on the board, but the one I would see in my house, the one who stood in the corner of my room and taunted me. I remember concentrating so hard to get it right. As I was working a nurse walked past me, and looked at my work, and said to me, "Wow, that is really good, how did you learn to draw like that?" My response was, "It's what I see in my bedroom." She just looked at me quite perplexed, smiled, and walked away. I just stood there staring at it for a long period of time until I felt someone take my hand, I looked up and it was my father and he said, "Come on Lisa, it is time to go." I grasped his hand tightly and we all walked out together. I did take one last look over my shoulder at the picture I drew as we were walking away, and that same nurse was just standing there staring at me, I smiled and put my head down and continued on my way.

Transition…

Once we were back home my dad took some time off from work. During that time he packed up all of my brothers belongings. I watched him packing with such anger and fury. At times he would stop sit on my brother's bed and just weep. Sometimes I would go in and sit next to him and hold his hand. He would squeeze it tight, and then kiss me lovingly on the forehead. He never said a word, just silently thanking me for being there. My mom was locked in her bedroom only coming out to use the bathroom. When I walked by the room all I could smell was heavy cigarette smoke. I felt it was like days before I saw her again. Everything felt abnormal and awkward. I just tried to move along with what was going on. Nothing felt good.

All of my brother's clothing, toys, and the big metal Tonka trucks that he loved so much were now all packed in big boxes. My dad started loading them up in the car and he said to me, "Lisa, let's take a ride together. I need your help." I asked him what we were doing with Jon Jon's things, and he told me we were going to an orphanage to donate them! I said to him, "Please do not take the matchbox cars away. Jon Jon and I love playing with them, and when he comes back that is the first thing we are going to do." My dad just stared at me, annoyed, and then he slowly put that box back in the garage.

I watched him walk into the garage, and place it on the step, and come back out. His head was down and he was pale. I remember the sad look on his face. I was still confused so I asked him again, "Daddy, why would we give Jon Jon's stuff away because when he comes back he will need them?" I got no response from him, not even a look, so I waited until we were in the car.

As we were pulling away from the house and driving up the road I asked the question for a third time, as I anxiously waited for an answer! My dad didn't even look at me, when he responded in a nasty tone, by saying, "Don't worry, he won't need them anymore, now let's just listen to the music and drive!" He startled me with his loud gruff tone, which made me jump out of my skin, so I remained silent for the whole ride as the look on his face said it all. I sadly looked out the window as we traveled along the roads.

I watched the sky, counted the clouds, and hummed softly to myself as the music played on. I had no idea where we were going, or what an orphanage really was, but my dad did mutter something about kids needing things and having no parents. I thought how odd, no parents? OK, what about brothers or sisters? I thought about many things as we traveled the long and winding roads to this strange place. I was a little scared, as in my imagination a jail came to mind. Children locked up because they didn't have families. I had this image in my head of the story of Hansel and Gretel. A picture from my book flashed across my mind of the children in these little wooden cages. It was distorted to me and I was upset by this. My stomach instantly had butterflies in it. My eyes felt tight and my vision spotty. I was instantly nervous.

Then I thought maybe we were bringing my brother's things there because that is where he will live now. He did say he was coming back to visit, or maybe he meant I had to go to this place called an orphanage to see him? I was totally confused, so I just waited until we got there to see what it was all about. Maybe Jon Jon will be there to greet us, but why would he want to live away from us? Oh maybe it was where the angels live at an orphanage? He did tell me the angels were coming for him, hmm… ok let's see!

When we got to where we were going we pulled into this long driveway with a huge parking lot. I helped my dad carry all of my brother's belongings inside this big building that looked more like a detention center than a home. I looked for my brother immediately, but he was not there. I was not happy about this at all, but as a child I did what I was told. I remained quiet and followed orders, as my mind raced feverishly. As we made our way inside, my eyes were wide as I scanned the scene feeling anxious and nervous. It felt cold and dark in there and I didn't like it at all. I remember this ugly mustard colored wallpaper on the walls with very dark wood. As I looked up at the ceiling there were cobwebs hanging down from the dimmed lights.

My dad was greeted by a tall blond woman with glasses, and I remember watching her and wondering where all the little children were. My mind floated back to the image of the wooden cages, but I pushed that thought away immediately! She was soft spoken, and I could not hear what she was saying. She spoke with my dad for a few moments while holding his hands, as I stood there looking around. She hugged him, and I heard her say, "I am so sorry for your loss, and thank you for your kindness." We left all the boxes right there in the hallway. Everything connected to my brother was just sitting there in this sad, old place. I was completely disturbed by this sight, and I had tears in my eyes. The woman looked at me with compassion in her eyes as tears slowly flowed down my cheeks. My dad took my hand and pulled me along as I reluctantly went with him looking over my shoulder until we were out the door and back in the car. Just like that, his personal items were gone. No further explanation was ever given, and I did not ask any questions. The car ride home was silent as well. Little tears continued to roll down my face as we pulled away from that building, and I remember looking out the window and up into the sky, hoping to see my brother's face. I whispered to myself, "Please come back to us."

The next day my dad went back to work.

As for my mom, she continually sat on the couch everyday crying, as she talked to herself and chain-smokes. It was unbearable. Once again I was alone. One morning, I decided to go outside on the front lawn to play like I used to do. It was a warm and sunny day. It felt good to be out of that house. The sun felt so warm on my face, and I felt so alive. Being in that house was awful. It felt totally dead to me. Our house was now filled with constant sorrow, and the continual sobs of my broken-down mother, which echoed down the hallways.

I was standing there looking around at the neighborhood taking it all in and thinking back to a time when all of us kids were running around playing tag through all the yards. Then suddenly I looked up into the sky like someone whispered in my ear and told me to do so. All of a sudden, everything became animated to me. The sky became extra bright, and all I could see around me was light. In the middle of that light was my brother Jon Jon. He told me not to be scared and that he loved me. He then went on to say he was sorry he had to go, and he was smiling. Then in a moment everything went back to normal, and he was gone.

That is when it really hit me. My brother was not coming back, he was gone forever, and he just came to say good-bye. How could he leave me alone like this? This house was scary! My mom was scary! My dad was always gone, and when he was home he was scary! I was alone, it hit me like a ton of bricks… I was six…. I became hysterical screaming and crying on the front lawn, my mom heard me and came out. She ran over to me and is tried to calm me down, but she could not. I was totally flipped out beyond belief. The devastation seemed to swallow me up, and I was out of control. I wanted my brother, do you hear me I want him back! Why did you have to take him from me? I was screaming this up to the sky over and over again pointing and clutching my little fist! My mother was trying to talk to me, and at first I did not even hear her. Lisa who are you talking to, who are you screaming at? I snapped back at her with tears in my eyes, the angels that took my brother! I am now screaming, Jon Jon, come back, come back, over and over again. My mom didn't know what to do, so she scooped me up in her arms, and ran down the street to my neighbor's house. I was kicking and screaming the whole way, totally out of control. I remember my arms and legs frantically moving wanting to get away. I was feeling trapped and claustrophobic and I could not breath. I wanted to jump up to heaven and take my brother back to where he belonged!

My mom was frightened by my behavior, and she was shaking all over. We got to my neighbors house and my mom was banging on the door with her foot screaming as she was holding me. At this point, she was frantic, and I am emotionally gone! I continued to kick and punch like I was fighting for my life. My neighbor finally comes to the door. We go into the house, and after what seemed like an eternity the neighbors finally help calm me down. From the moment my mother scooped me up into her arms until I was calm again, I do not remember too much of anything except the loud sounds of myself screaming, and my body wiggling out of control. That is the image that stays in my mind when I think back to that moment. It was a total loss of control. In that moment every emotion inside of me blew up like a bomb, with no prior warning.

When it was finally over we walked back home hand in hand silently. I remember looking around at the neighborhood at all the houses and trees, and nothing seemed the same to me. It all seemed foreign, like I was transported to a different place. I was confused, and felt lost. When we reached my house we both slowly made our way up the stairs and went inside. It felt like my mom did not want to go back in there as we slowly took each step. I could hear her breathing heavy, reluctant to move forward. I was exhausted, and distraught. I went into my room alone. My mom did not follow me she just stood in the kitchen and lit up a cigarette. I then lay down on my bed and sleep. The incident was never talked about again!

I do not even think my mom ever told my dad what happened. He never said a word to me about it, nor did I ever hear my parents discuss it. Years later I mentioned the incident to my dad, and he seemed oblivious to what I was talking about. That bothered me to think that something so traumatic happened to me, and my dad had never been told.

My parents did not know how to communicate with each other at all. They never did. From the moment they met it was a dysfunctional relationship. Is it possible that they may have briefly discussed the incident? I don't think so because my father seemed totally in the dark about it. If it was actually talked about I am sure it was not something they spent much time on, so maybe he just forgot. So much was happening at that time I am sure being so overwhelmed with grief, a lot of things were just blocked out!

My parents didn't know how to express their emotions, and that is sad. When I think back to all the things they were going through as a couple trying to keep their young family intact, they were always silent with each other. I do not remember them ever sitting at the table having conversation about anything. My mother was always busy doing her thing, and he was off taking care of business. He would come home and the silence was endless. He would tell her what to do, and she would do it. My parents were together but alone at the same time. We all had something in common, and didn't even know it.

The entire time that my brother was ill, they never discussed that either. How is it that he could have been so sick and they didn't even talk about the future possibility that he could die? They certainly never talked to him and me about it, that was for sure! My brother and I discussed it with each other on several occasions, but our parents never noticed. As children, we were more in tune to what was going on than the adults.

My parents definitely did not know how to talk to me, because they never really did. After my brother's death, there was always a lot of uneasy silence. Everything was always left unsaid, and empty. There was always tension in the house, and everything was always pushed under the rug and never discussed.

I was one sad, confused little girl, and nobody thought to ask the questions.

ALONE I WEEP

Looking out the window lonely as can be,
How could my family up and leave me?

Just a little girl with fear in her eyes,
How could these grown folks straight up
Lie?

Standing there small and frail, how could
This child prevail...

Windows with bars to keep her inside,
Frozen in fear, wanting to run and hide...

All alone, yes she is!! Learning to hold it
All in...

See what these bars have taught thee, never
Let your feelings out. Never be free...

Cold and alone, on this dark day, wanting
To run, going astray...

Too little to understand what dangers hold
Deep, alone in this nightmare never peaceful
Sleep...

Wanting to scream out rid this pain.
Wanting comfort from family.
Please stop the rain...

Alone I stand sealing my fate, closing my
Doors to family, is it too late?

CHAPTER 3
Loss

Chapter 3

Loss

FROM AGE 6 TO 10 life as an only child was challenging. After my brother's death my home life changed drastically. My dad worked all the time late into the night, and every weekend. When he was not working he was card playing, gambling, and drinking. He also bartended and was a bouncer. During the spring and summer, he was on a softball team, and we spent the day at the bar after the game was over. I believe he did anything that he could do not to be home.

On Sundays during the fall and winter, we would spend time with family, my grandparents, aunts and uncles, and cousins. Our family dinners consisted of the men drinking, smoking, betting on the football games, and playing cards. The women would sit around the table smoking and drinking coffee, while there were endless trays of food being prepared. The kids would run around and play, and we were considerably wild. We were offered wine at a young age, as this was Italian tradition. You would think that the wine would slow us down, but that was certainly not the case! As kids we were not angels, we would sneak into my grandfather's room and look through his stash of Penthouse magazines. We would examine the pages wide-eyed, opening up to the centerfolds giggling and laughing. Wow Miss December, my cousin said, and we just all busted out in hysterics. We always managed to have a great time together, and there was a lot of laughter.

At times I would sleep at either of my grandparents' houses as my mom was a mess 24/7. After my brother's death she was so depressed all the time. Her behavior was bizarre. She would go from one extreme to the next, cycling as quickly as one could turn the page in a book. At times she was scary, and I was left alone with her, not knowing what to do.

My memories of my mom are of her sitting on the couch smoking and crying. She would talk to herself and play music. At times she would argue with herself and swear a lot. I always wondered whom she was talking to because I didn't see anyone standing there. Then there were her manic episodes when she would be loud and boisterous. She would laugh and dance around the kitchen, which always ended up with her wetting her pants and the floor. She would dance in her own urine and seemed to love every minute of it. It was like she was doing a dance of mental freedom. This was very hard for me to watch!

At times, she would be up all night cleaning like a mad woman. She would take everything out of the kitchen cabinets, wash them down, and put them back. Some nights she would take things off the walls, and rearrange them using a hammer and nails, continually switching them around into different places. There were also nights when she would not sleep at all and she was loud, talking to herself repeating things like, "I need to fix it, I need to fix it," or "It's not clean enough," over and over again. She would continually smoke through this whole process. I remember one night she decided to repaint the whole kitchen, and when I woke up in the morning I thought I was the crazy one! As a child this was frightening. I didn't know quite what to make of it all, but I was intelligent enough to know something was very wrong. I knew that fresh paint and furniture being rearranged daily was out of the ordinary.

I also know that my mom being up all night doing these things was not normal.

Then, she would say unusual things to me all the time. I never knew what was going to come out of her mouth next. I remember one night, I was sitting there watching TV and she said, "Hey Lisa!" I replied, "What, Mom?"

"Remember once you lift your dress, you always lift your dress!"

I just looked at her and said, "OK," and then said to myself, *what is she talking about I don't even wear dresses!* The conversations that we had most of the time were her saying bizarre things, and me trying to figure them out. It was like a sick game of cat and mouse. I never knew where I stood with her as I could hardly keep up with her cycles.

When my dad would come home most of the time he was drunk, and they would fight terribly. She would wait for him to come in the door, and start on him immediately. She would make him so crazy that he would smash and break things all over the house. My mom seemed to relish in the chaos, and would be foul-mouthed and glare at him like she wanted him dead. He never hit her, but broke everything around her. When the rage was over he would go to bed, and she would continue to sit stewing in her misery. It was devastating as a child to witness this night after night. I was totally traumatized. I was always on edge, and nervous waiting for the next disaster to happen. Sometimes I would get spacey and daydream, going into my own little fantasy world. I realize now looking back it was my way of trying to cope with all these traumatic events that continued to implode in my life every day.

On the occasions when my dad would not come home drunk, we did have a few family dinners together, and when that happened, we would have to sit in silence. One night my dad stabbed his fork into my mother's hand because she went to take a piece of meat that he wanted. He sternly said, "Don't touch it!" He had this angry glare in his eyes, and all I could see was contempt for her. She just looked him square in the eye and said, "Fucking choke on it!" I just sat there and took it all in like always. I was trying to understand why my parents would act this way towards each other. I felt the animosity and disgust between them, but I couldn't understand why they would hate each other so much. I would think of my friends' parents and how they acted towards each other, and they were nothing like mine. I would never express to my friends what was happening in my household, but I was always appreciative when I was invited to eat over at their house for dinner.

When I went to bed at night, I would lie there and wait, most of the time scared out of my mind. There were strange noises in my room and shadow figures in the corner. I would try to ignore them, but they never went away, always taunting me until I had enough. Sometimes I would put the covers over my head, but most of the time I would end up in my parents' bed out of fear. As soon as I went into my room at night it would begin. I would try to stay brave, and tough it out. I did not want it to win, but fear over took me, and I was tired. I do remember that most nights it got the best of me, and yes, I would go running. This angered me, as I wanted to feel comforted in my own room, but I could not. This was another obstacle in my life that was terrifying and confusing. There was nowhere for me to run or hide, someone or something was always at my heels.

On some occasions my dad would come home drunk and lie across my bed and talk to me, slurring his words asking me if I loved my daddy. "Please love me," he would say, and I would respond with, "OK, Daddy, I will love you always." I wanted to help him somehow, but I didn't know what to do. I was just a child wanting to be cared for, but in this case it was the opposite. Then when he was done talking, he would fall asleep snoring so loudly I could not hear myself think! Even back then he was looking for my love and support. He needed me. He wanted me to make it better, but I could not. How could I? What pressure to be put under as a small child, feeling like you have to fix things so beyond your control. It was unbearable, but I had no choice but to endure it. Once he was asleep, that is when I would make my escape to my mom's room. This was some escape, the lesser of the two evils. All I wanted to do was to sleep peacefully. I just wanted to feel safe and calm, but I never did. There was always chaos and dysfunction. It was the unknown that was the worst. I never knew what would happen next. When I would finally fall asleep I would have terrible nightmares, ones that were even more terrifying than my parents and that awful house.

My mom would get up during the night and smoke and eat. I would follow her because I was scared to be alone. I would see things in her room as well, and my dreams were frightening. I would cry sitting there because I was so tired and begged her to come to bed, but she would not until she was finished. Most of the time she would sit in silence and ignore my crying. Once in a while she would become agitated and say things like, "Lisa, stop crying or I will smash your face."

I would say, "OK, Mommy," as I whimpered, trying to pull myself together.

"You always cry, you are such a brat. Your brother cried because he was dying he had a reason to cry but you don't so just shut up!"

I would just look at her with my big blue eyes and tears would flow. I looked like a scared little bunny rabbit, wide eyed and motionless. I would then remain silent and just wait. This was a cycle that was repeated night after night.

I do remember at times when my dad was actually home longer than a moment; we would bond by watching a movie like *Bonnie and Clyde* or *The Godfather*. This further traumatized me and enhanced my fears. I think my dad thought it was ok for me to watch these violent movies with him, because in his eyes we were spending quality time together. Maybe it made him feel better about not being there most of the time. Maybe it eased his guilt, as he knew being home alone with my mom was awful! We would also watch boxing and football, during which my dad would get so angry he would scream and throw things towards the TV. He would always startle me with his loud abrasive tones, and scare me when he got violent. I learned quite quickly to remain quiet and just observe. It was safer that way, until the chaos passed. In the midst of it all there was my mother once again sitting on the couch in the other room smoking, staring into space. This was our family time.

Back in the 70s it was common for therapy groups to be done in the home. The resources for the mentally ill were limited, and being sick was not publicly talked about. My mother was struggling terribly so her doctor thought this type of group would be helpful for her. My parents agreed to this, so my mom did have a therapy group that would come to our house once a week. I remember her therapist, Mrs. Barker. She was a tall black woman, with a very sweet smile. She was a warm person, and always dressed to a tee. Oddly enough, I remember her pocket books always matched her outfits. I thought that was so cool. She reminded me of a black Barbie doll.

She was always so kind to me, and gave me a lot of attention every time she came. I enjoyed talking to her, and actually looked forward to seeing her. I remember that I was becoming quite comfortable with her and one day I decided to share this story...

THE 1965 MUSTANG

On one sunny afternoon in the spring, I was sitting on my front step just thinking. I was bored and desperate for attention. My mom was in the house as usual and oddly none of the kids in the neighborhood were out, but the reality of that was they should not of been out because they were all in school. At times my mother would randomly keep me home from school because she would be terrified that I was going to die! She would tell me this, "Lisa, if you leave the house today you will be dead. Do you hear me?" I would say ok and just shake my head in frustration because I knew I was stuck home with her all day, when I could be at school having fun with my friends. This really stressed me out a lot!

So there I was thinking, and what I came up with was I was going to prove a point to her. I would take her car, go for a joy ride, and come back. I will show her I am not going to die today! My mom had a beautiful 1965 Mustang. It was gold with tan leather interior. It was in mint condition, and it flew! Everyone loved this car, and she got a lot of attention with it, which she loved.

I go in the house looking for her, and she was in the bathroom. I anxiously grab her keys and run out the door as fast as I could. I go to the car, thinking how hard could this be, I watched my mom do it all the time! I get in and pull the seat up. I could barely see over the dashboard and my feet just touched the pedals. I put the key in start the engine, drop it in drive and floor it! The car peeled out and swerved a bit on a dirt patch, and with a cloud of dust I was off.

The excitement that I felt was such a rush. No fear! I flew down the road, turned the car around, and came back up the street. As I passed my house my mom was coming out the front door, as she must have heard the noise. I knew I was in trouble, so I turned it around at the top of my road and came rolling in to park it. I knew I was in deep poop, as I thought, but I was alive. As I got out of the car to explain myself, my mom grabbed me before I could mutter a word and beat the shit out of me right on the front lawn. She was cursing and screaming as she dragged me in the house by my long hair. I was shaking in fear as she continued to smash me over and over again. I was so terrified that I do not remember what she was saying to me, I just remember hands flying and screaming.

When it was over I sat in the corner of my room, curled up in a ball and quivering for what seemed like hours. When I finally had the courage to emerge from my hiding spot, she was sitting at the kitchen table glaring at me. I slowly walked by her and sat on the couch to watch TV. I was praying that she would not start up again, and she didn't, but her stares were just as disturbing…

After this story, Mrs. Barker did go on to tell both my parents that I needed counseling because she could see I was in total distress. She spoke of the incident with the car, and my dad seemed to be clueless of my little adventure, as my mom stood next to him spewing nastiness at him trying to change the subject. Mrs. Barker saw in me what nobody else even noticed. I know this is why I liked her so much. This woman that I really didn't know saw me, and she noticed me. The damaged me! She wanted to help me, and I had a glimmer of hope. I remember the look of horror on her face as I nervously told her my story. I felt maybe she was the one to save me.

Well, my glimmer was short lived. My father flipped out and told her if she spoke of it again she would be kicked out of our house forever. He said, "You are here to deal with my wife, not my daughter. She is off limits!" My dad didn't believe in the whole mental illness thing and hated the thought of my mom being on medicine, so he put it down all the time, which made it worse for her. He also put her down for gaining weight. He harassed her all the time about being sick, and being fat because of her medications. He did not understand her at all. My mother had NO support when she needed it the most.

In my mother's defense she never really had any help. My aunt who lived behind us would come into our home and ridicule her and say get up off that couch, there is nothing wrong with you, or your house is dirty—clean it! Stop taking those meds. You are getting as fat as a cow.

I remember this quite clearly. My mother was always put down for her behaviors. There was no positive support or re-enforcement.

Instead of people trying to understand or help her, they made it worse. My grandmother Theresa and my Aunt Cathy would do the same things. Also, our neighbor Edna was another culprit who was good for bashing and running. I feel in their minds they all thought they were being helpful, and trying to get my mom to move or be motivated, but there was truly no understanding about her illness and very little compassion. It is sad to think this is how people do treat the mentally ill, especially how they did back then. I was just a child and I was becoming more aware of things and feeling extremely angry about how people would treat my mother. I was so confused about so many things and felt totally alone. Nobody understood her or me ,for that matter. The only person who had asked questions or offered help was shot down immediately by my dad. I was allowed to stay home with my mom and endure her crazy behaviors.

My family definitely had their shortcomings, and their thought processes were a bit warped. I remember being at my grandma Theresa's house for dinner with the family. My uncle who lived behind us raised rabbits. He had rabbits that were pets, and ones that he would slaughter and sell. My uncle did give me a rabbit, and I would go over every day and feed it, along with my cousins and play with it. It was my pet! Well that night during the big family dinner, my uncle announced that the chicken in sauce that we were eating was actually rabbit from his stock.

I was upset, of course—as kids you do not want to think of a rabbit as dinner. Also, I would go over there every day and play with all of them. Then my uncle looked at me and said, "Lisa, this is your rabbit, and he is dinner tonight!" I looked at him in disbelief and horror. The words were echoing in my ears over and over again, as I was in total shock. My whole family started laughing at me, and seemed to get quite a kick out of it. I said, "Uncle Will, you are joking, right?"

He looked me square in the eyes and said, "No joke, sweetie. Say hello to Sonny."

I got up, and ran from the table and went to the bathroom and threw up. I was hysterical, and everyone continued to laugh, as more wine was being poured.

My mother was the only one who said something. I could hear her screaming from the bathroom calling them every swear word you could imagine and more. My mom the one who was labeled sick with mental illness was the only one to stand up for me, and be rational for once. I think I stayed in the bathroom for the rest of dinner, and when I finally came out I lay on my grandfather's bed and just cried. I was so hurt and I sobbed for what seemed like forever. It was like losing my brother all over again. Someone or something that I loved so tremendously was ripped from my world without a moment's notice, and I was left alone. Talk about being traumatized! That was a big one, as I only had few enjoyments to break up the dysfunction. Another one was just taken away from me in a very twisted fashion. I was distraught.

Everyone considered my mother to be the crazy one, and she was, but she was not alone!

AS TIME WENT ON IT JUST GOT WORSE…

Out of the blue, my mom decided one day that she would change my bedroom to my brother's old room. She couldn't stand looking at it anymore, and wanted it erased. My parents redid the whole thing over, and made my old room a playroom. I hated the fact that I was now in my brother's old room. It was too hard for me to be in there. Even though his belongings were gone and it was brand new again, the memories we shared could never be erased with a new coat of paint or wallpaper! My parents never even asked me if it was OK to move me in there, they just did it! This traumatized me even more. How could they move me without even asking?

They took the little bit of security that I had and ripped it away. Even though at night I was scared in my room, during the day it was my little happy place to get away from reality. Now, I had this beautiful new room to be in, but all I wanted was to be in my playroom. I felt comforted in there as I had a great imagination and would play alone for hours with my dolls and my music. It was my escape from reality. When I went in there nothing else mattered. I did have friends in the neighborhood that I would go out and play with and at those times, I almost forgot what was going on in my world. I loved being out of that house, and as I got a little older I found any reason to go out. Then at the end of the day, back in I went wondering what horrors would I have to face? There were so many moments of dysfunction. The stories are endless. Day in and day out, year after year, and here is another one of those magical moments…

The Sex Talk, Joann Style...

As life was always challenging for me on a daily basis, why should this day be any different? I could not have been more than ten years old at the time. I was happily playing in my room with my Barbie dolls. I remember sitting on the floor, dressing them, talking with them, being in my own little fantasy world. It always felt good to travel in my mind.

It was a warm summer day and the breeze was coming through my window, and my neighbor was mowing his lawn. The smell of the fresh-cut grass came flowing through my room like a melody of peacefulness. The intoxicating smell made me extremely happy. Sitting there with my legs crossed Indian-style, as Barbie and Ken, were about to go off to the ball together, I was smiling. I had a fabulous imagination, and it took me to far away places with many great adventures. In my fantasy world I was so far away from my mother and that is where I found my moments of serenity!

Then my moment was over. There standing in the door way was my mother. She was staring down at me, and I felt so small. My throat got instantly dry, and my forehead crinkled, as I was not sure which Joann I was going to see. I was just silent and waiting for her outburst. She came into my room and went right over to the window. She was watching the neighbor mow his lawn, and she said to me, "Oh Lisa, look at Gary mowing that lawn. He is so hot and sweaty." I was instantly grossed out, but remained silent hoping she would just make her way back out! After all she was ruining my time! Why does my fantasy world have to be invaded by this mean and nasty giant? She was stomping out all of my pure thoughts and actions that were occurring right before her very essence stunk up the place!

"Lisa!! Are you listening to me????"

I heard my mother's voice, and I was shaken back into the moment. I said, "Yes, Mom. I hear you!" Honestly, I'd blanked out for a few moments because I just didn't want to do that dance, but she was going to make it happen, twist away!

"Lisa, let me tell you something. Listen carefully to me. See Gary next door? He has a big hard on for me, and he is sweating because he wants me!"

OK, he wants you for what? This was me thinking, as she continued.

"I tell you he wants me." Then she screamed out my bedroom window, "Gary! Gary, you want a piece of this!!!"

I do not think he could hear here because of the lawn mower, or he chose to ignore her, so she turned her attention back onto me.

"Fuck him, he can't take a joke! Lets talk about sex!"

I said, "Mom, what about sex, and what does that mean?" I had no clue, I was so naive to all of it, I just wanted to be a kid and play with my dolls.

"Well let me tell you about sex," she said. "You need to know, it is important. Your father and I do it all the time. He takes his penis and shoves it in my twat!"

Then, I was totally twisted and confused. I did not quite get what she was saying to me. It definitely was not registering in my innocent brain. I have heard her say these words before in anger, but not like this. So I said, "Mom, what is a twat, and is a penis part of my dad and why would he put it inside of you?" She was still standing over me, and I felt so tiny and helpless sitting on the floor holding my dolls as she gave me that one-eyed stare of hers.

I got a pit in my stomach, and I instantly stiffened up, but I just waited. My mom came over in a violent rage and ripped my dolls out of my hand, and started tearing their clothing off with a vengeance. I was mortified as I watched her so enraged with my dolls in hand. She started spewing vulgar words at me like cunt, dick, fucking, as she took my two dolls and smashed them together in a sexual movement with such force that my Barbie's head popped off! I instantly started crying which made her even angrier so she slapped my face screaming at me to stop. As I lay there curled up in a ball, she started in again.

She went on to say this to me, "Lisa, sex is a man and woman fucking, do you hear me? Fucking, nasty dirty sex! Your father wants to stick his dick in my twat all the time, and then he wants to put it in my mouth, do you hear me!"

I wanted to just get up and run away but I didn't, I knew better. I just sat there and took it all in, as she was so large and animated in her movements. She then said that all this white stuff (as she called it) comes out everywhere and she was supposed to be happy about it, but she was not, she hated it, but it was her duty as a wife.

I was dumbfounded by this whole conversation, and completely confused. Of course in typical Joann fashion she flipped like a switch and started laughing hysterically, and said her famous line, "Lighten up, Lisa. You don't know how to take a joke."

And with that she started to walk away. I sat back up slowly, but she turned back around to throw my dolls in my face. "I hope I do not ever see you make your dolls have sex, do you hear me??"

With my head down, I said to her, "OK, Mommy, I won't."

"Good girl, Lisa. You know mommy loves you."

I said, "I know," and she walked out the door singing some crazy tune she just made up in her head.

I was ten sitting on my floor holding my dolls…and the beat goes on…

In the good weather, my dad would play softball on Sunday mornings. I would go with him to watch, and we would always end up at the bar afterwards. My mom would come sometimes, but she hated the bar and drinking. This bar is a place that will be burned in my memory forever. My first bar experience, at only 9 years old. After his games we were supposed to go to my Grandma Theresa's for lunch, as she would cook every Sunday. As time went on we would get there later and later. There was always a fight. My grandmother hated the bar. Half of the time we would take the food and go home because they would fight so badly. Then my grandmother started insisting that we come to dinner on Tuesday and Thursday nights as well. My mom detested this, but we were forced to go by my dad. There were always issues and problems. Half of the time, my dad would not show up, but we always did—my father's orders! My Aunt Cathy was always mean to my mom, and my grandmother as well. My grandfather on the other hand was the only kind one in the bunch. Nobody knew how to handle my mother's mental illness. Instead of trying to understand her, they verbally abused her. It was hard to stand by and witness this and feel so defenseless. I did want to help my mother, but I did not know how. I hated the way they treated her. I wanted to scream at all of them, but I remained silent as I was taught. This went on over the next couple of years.

Of course my mom would say bizarre things to me all the time, which made it even worse. We would be sitting there and she would say, "Lisa, your Aunt Cathy is gay, do you hear me?"

"Yes, Mom. I am listening."

"A lesbian, I tell you, a lesbian. Do not be alone with her ever or you will turn into one too."

"Mom, what are you saying?"

"I am saying your Grandma Theresa looks like George Washington."

"Sure, Mom, whatever you say!"

"Did you hear me, Lisa?"

"Yes I did, Mom."

"Don't forget or you will die tonight."

"I promise, Mom, I will not forget."

"Good girl, my beautiful blue-eyed angel from heaven!"

That is how many of our conversations went. I did not know what to make of some of the things that she said so I would just agree.

The family unit was now in total dysfunction, and by age 11 my parents spent absolutely no time together. We did manage to go on a few vacations together. We would always have to take my Aunt Cathy along for some unknown reason. In those moments as a child, I felt like for a brief time everything was ok and we were a happy family. When we were driving in the car I would fantasize about going to a big castle in the mountains and I was a princess. In this fantasy everyone loved me and my family was happy. We had everything in this castle, and my brother was with us. When those special times were over, reality set in. Once we were home again, it was always a great disappointment.

We did also manage to go camping a couple of times with family friends, which I enjoyed because I was outside and felt freedom. At those times, wandering around exploring the woods was very exciting to me, and I felt close to my brother. We used to explore together all the time. My dad actually seemed to enjoy the outdoors as well, and we had some special moments to bond. Of course, my mom hated it, and sat in the screened tent smoking. We all joked that at least she was being useful by keeping the bugs away with her cigarettes! Once we got home it was always back to the same thing. My dad would run, and my mom would sit and cry.

At this point my dad was working in New York. At times he would take me to work on Saturdays with him. I enjoyed that a lot. He also started cheating on my mother with different women, and even at that young age I was aware of the way women he worked with treated him. I knew he was cheating even at age 11. Mym knew too. She never said anything to him but she knew. She said it to me instead…

The conversation went like this…

"Hey, Lisa!"

"Yes, Mom?"

"When you go to work with your father tell those bitches if they keep it up their skin will peel off."

"What did you just say?"

"You heard me! Every woman your father touches, their skin will peel off! Warn them!"

"Mom, I don't think I will say that," I stuttered a little.

"Yes you will, and if you don't, I will know and then you will be punished by God! Say it, do you hear me? Say it! Now! Repeat it back to me NOW," she screamed.

"Ok, Ok, Mommy. If you bitches keep it up your skin will peel off. Don't let my dad touch you." I was shaking, not making eye contact with her, as I did not know how she would react. I just waited.

She finally said, "Yes, good girl. You are mommy's angel."

My mom's behavior was getting worse for sure. My parent's relationship was done. They were going through the motions, and I was quite aware of that too. I was growing up with all this knowledge in my head, all these thoughts and questions with nobody to talk to. Can you imagine having all these thoughts and feelings rolling around in your head and never being able to verbalize them? They taunted me! I felt so unloved and alone. I felt worthless and invisible. It was like I didn't matter!

My parents would try to take brief moments to be with me and then they were gone again. It was more painful to have those brief moments, because when they were gone I always related it to my brother dying. Those same thoughts and feelings were in my heart and in my head, but my mouth remained silent. I longed for my parents to be my parents, and that was just not the case. I felt I had to take care of myself. I was so lonely and lost. I was a sad, sad little girl and nobody even took notice…

ℭℜ LOSS ℜℭ

Loss—what a big meaning for such a small word..

One has to gain to lose
One has to lose, to find hope!

Once all is lost, you can start to gain...
Gain, hope and strength
Gain a new beginning, put closure in its
Proper place...

Mourn the loss... Process this deep sense
Of sorrow, the meaning behind the loss...

Ask, Was it for the better?
Why do I have to feel such pain?
What am I to gain?

Then move forward, keep this deficit
Close to the heart... This your battle scar,
A medal of honor, your personal keepsake
For all of time...

This to remind you: keep you humble...
Learn to grow from this personal defeat, which
Holds you down for a moment...

Then nature's wrath takes its course. A rush of
Release pushes you forward, forcing you to
Move on....
Make amends, Make peace....
This is the process we call LIFE!!!

Lisa Zarcone

CHAPTER 4
Silent Tears

Chapter 4

Silent Tears

At age 11... I was in 6th grade.

Everyone remembers 6th grade! This is when junior high begins, and all the kids go from being buddies on the play ground to becoming quite critical of one another. This is when the pairing up of groups begins, and sadly some are left on the sidelines to become loners walking the halls of shame. This very awkward time in one's life that feels uncomfortable and strange to all. Is anyone really accepted, or are we trying to play the parts of this emotionally charged game of the teen years?

The self-awareness of our bodies and thoughts are changing rapidly, and everyone wants to be at the top of their game. The boys are starting to look at girls in a very different light, and the girls begin to get giddy as puberty hits! The bottom line is that nobody wants to stand out like a sore thumb, and everyone wants to be popular!

My mom is now becoming progressively worse as she has stopped taking her medications. I was starting to become embarrassed of her behavior. The kids in school would always make fun of me. I was tormented all the time. My mom would come to the school for any reason that she could make up. The principal didn't know what to make of her, so she allowed her to come and go as often as she liked! I would have to say the principal felt bad for her, as she knew my brother and how his death affected the school staff, as well as his classmates.

The last thing that I wanted was to have my mom show up and embarrass me. If she didn't actually come into the school or onto the playground, she would drive by at lunchtime, beep the horn, and scream out the window, "Lisa!!!!!" Everyone would always look at me and point, laughing and joking, pretending to be my mother, and scream my name. I would want to die in that moment every time it happened. I wanted to crawl in a hole and never come out. Sometimes, I would take notice of the aides or teachers supervising us, and they were laughing too. I would then put my head down and walk away. I did have a couple of friends who would come and try to console me, but other than that there was no compassion in junior high school.

My mom also started taking interest in the young boys in my class. Steven and Larry were her two favorites. Steven reminded her of my brother, as did every young boy! She would invite them over to my house all the time to hang out with me, but it was really all for her. She also did this with other kids in my class who were, let's say the outcasts of the classroom. My mom had a knack for choosing the most troubled and disturbed people to welcome into our home. For example there was a young girl named Anna who was having sex with everyone in the sixth grade. She was riddled with issues. Annette was mentally ill just like her. My mother always told me to be extra kind to them, and be their friend. The truth was I was in sixth grade and the last thing I wanted to be was labeled disturbed or troubled, but the labels I received as time went on in my life would be much worse.

Of course there were always boys. She loved the boys! That was all she talked about. She invited them over every day, and even let them drive her car to lure them in. I hated this and told her I didn't want them over, but she didn't care. She wanted them around. She loved the chaos. I remember one-day Steven's mom showed up at our house, and had an intense conversation with my mother in regards to her obsession with him. Of course she denied any such thing, and put the blame on me, stating that I needed to have my friends around. I do not believe his mother bought that story for a moment, and from that point on, she always gave my mother a hard time. They had many verbal arguments over it, and eventually he was not allowed to come over anymore.

My embarrassment grew daily. There was always something happening, and she was a master at creating chaos to get attention. To my dismay, she would go into my room and take my things, and give them away all the time. At one point it seemed like my classmates had more of my things than I did. I would cry and get so angry with her. I would confront her and yell, but she would always say, "You have enough stuff! You didn't need it anyways."

This is how many of our conversations would play out:

"Mom where is my glass pony that was on my dresser?" I asked "Oh that old thing, I gave it away to that girl in your class" she responds. "That was my favorite you know that, why would you give it away?" "Oh Lisa stop complaining you have everything a girl could want and more, stop being a greedy little pig!" " I am not being greedy mom, I just hate when you give my things away its not fair, and you seem to care more about strangers than you do about ME!"

When I spoke up to her she would become livid!

When she got angry, and was ready to explode she would give me this look of death, a glare that would go right through me from my head to the tip of my toes! I would feel her rage while standing there motionless waiting for her to implode! Then it would happen—she would let loose with her wicked tongue, and give it to me both barrels.

"I will tell you what is not fair Lisa, your dead brother laying in a casket right now in the ground all bones! That is not fair. His rotting corpse filled with maggots, that is not fair! Life is not fair I tell you, life is not fair!" She waved her fist at me, while screaming this over and over again. I looked at her in horror and ran to my room crying, and all I could hear was her eerie laughter in the background.

So my embarrassment grew, along with my anger. My mom would seek out any misfit and have them come over for a visit. I would come home from school and find strangers in my house all the time, even homeless bums off the street. Young, old, it didn't matter to her, she wanted to be surrounded by dysfunction twenty-four hours a day, seven days a week. She would even pick up hitchhikers, and bring them to our house. She would pull out money and cigarettes and give them to whomever she felt needed it! She put us in a great deal of danger without even knowing it.

I remember how some of these derelicts would look at me up and down devouring me with their eyes. Their stench filled the air, the filth on their ragged clothing rubbing on our white couch turned my stomach, as they would look at me waiting for a moment to pounce. At those moments I would look over at my mother who was talking a mile a minute, racing, manic-laughing, and joking. Then she would put on music and dance around the living room. I would retreat to my room, as I was terrified as to what they would do to me.

One time, one of the bums went to use the bathroom, and eventually wandered down the hall to my room. I turned around to see him standing in my doorway groaning and touching himself. My mom came down the hall and called him back into the living room. If she didn't come at that moment, you could only image what would have happened to me. I feel my brother was definitely watching over me that day for sure.

As all of this was unfolding, my dad was obviously absent. He would hear things second hand from the neighbors all the time, and he would get angry, but my mom could not have cared less about what he thought anymore! My dad was classic, he would come home yell and scream, and then leave. He never stayed around long enough to stop the madness. My dad just kept on running.

The Return of Jerry...

One day a young man came into the neighborhood his name was Jerry. He's been an old friend of my brother's back when they were little. He had dark hair and big blue eyes. He was not overly tall, but he was quite slender. At first glance he looked like an angel, but he was definitely the devil in disguise.

When they were little, they would play in the yard all the time with my brother's Tonka trucks. One day when they were playing in the yard, he decided to pull a knife out on my brother, acting all crazy and threatening for no apparent reason. At that point, he was kicked out of the neighborhood, never to be seen again. He moved away to New York shortly after that incident, but now he was back.

He came to our door that very day and told my mother he was sorry about what he did to my brother. My mother was excited to have a new young man to give her attention to and to hang out with, and it seemed like she forgot about the past, or didn't even care about what he did. She happily invited him to sit on the front step to talk about life. I could hear voices from the other room, and came closer to see who was here. I spotted this young man sitting there, and immediately recognized him from the past. He was sitting there all cocky and full of himself as he talked to her about my brother, and how bad he felt about his death. I knew he was lying from the moment I laid eyes on him, and I instantly hated him. I wanted no part of him, as far as I was concerned, he was scum. I remember standing in the doorway, peering through the screen listening to his lies, and feeling total contempt! My mother, on the other hand, loved the attention and told him to come back any time, and of course he did. This was his invitation to take advantage of a bad situation. Every time he showed up he would always try to talk to me but I ignored him. I knew he was no good, and I had a sick feeling in my stomach every time he came into our house. It was like I had a premonition of what was to come.

At this age I was still very childlike and immature. I loved to play with my dolls and I had no interest in boys. My mother, on the other hand, had other ideas in her head and pushed the issue of me liking boys. She wanted me to be with them, and she talked about it all the time. She stated to me during several of our conversations, that I had to have a boyfriend. She said it was time, and I needed to get moving. I told her I did not want a boyfriend, and she went through the roof, and accused me of being gay like my aunt. She demanded that I find a boyfriend soon, or she would find one for me. She was adamant about the topic and was determined to get her way.

My father told my mom that he did not want Jerry around. He said he was a bad kid, and he reminded her of what he did to my brother, and said his return would only cause trouble for us. He did not want Jerry around me for sure, as he did not trust him. My dad had the right instincts, but lacked the drive to follow through on what he would say. He would shout and demand, then leave again. As always this was his classic move. Of course she did not listen, because he never did anything about anything, he just bantered. So my mother moved forward and invited Jerry over any chance she got. As for my dad, he was never home to save me from what was to become the worst year and a half of my life…

Two things happened immediately….

My mom wanted me to have a party, which I did not want. She invited all these kids I didn't like, and all these boys. They came in my home, and made fun of me for having my dolls set up in my play room, and my mom encouraged us to play spin the bottle. It was a total disaster.

This was the first time I kissed a boy. I didn't even want to… I could hear my mother yelling in the background, "Kiss the boys, yes kiss the boys!" I was livid. I knew if I didn't do it there would be hell to pay after, so I just did it to make her happy. I hated every moment of it, and wanted it all just to be over. I wanted everyone to leave! When the house was finally empty, my mom proceeded to get all revved up, dancing around the house, and talking crazy. She was insisting that I have a boyfriend! I told her I did not want one, and she slapped me across the face, and said "Too bad, you're getting one, and you will like it!" Once again, feeling defeated and unheard, I retreated to my room and cried myself to sleep.

The next day, I packed up all my dolls and what little part of my child hood and innocence that was left. Now it was truly all gone. This is something I didn't want to do but was forced to. I was angry as another part of my fantasy world was pulled away and I was then facing my new reality. My mom continually invited kids to my home. It was a revolving door of teenagers. Sometimes I would go to my room to be alone, and she would be in the living room entertaining them with her crazy antics. She would start to sing and dance, and they would laugh at her. I could hear the echoing down the hall, and I just wanted to escape. I could not believe that they actually enjoyed her company. I guess they tolerated her wild and out of control behavior, as it gave them somewhere to be.

I started roller-skating to get away from her, but she would come with me and made friends with the owner. My mom always put herself into a position to be around young boys…I knew it, and I hated it… There was no escape from her torment…I was suffocating.

The next thing that happened was Jerry! He was relentless. He would show up all the time and my mom would let him in. He told her he had leukemia like my brother and needed help. That was it, his key in, and his moment to prey upon me. He constantly said things to me. He was stalking me, hunting me down like a defenseless fawn. Taking his opportunity, going in for the kill, so to speak.

"You are now my girlfriend, and I am in charge of your home. Your dad hates you. I am the only one who cares about you."

I looked at him and said, "Jerry I hate you and want nothing to do with you. I will not date you over my dead body."

His response, "That could be arranged." I just looked at him, and said nothing.

Day in and day out he would say these things to me over and over again. My mom was no help as she kept pushing him on me. "Lisa, date him, Lisa, be with him…"

I was 12… My mom would also let him drive her car. He was only 15. She would let all the other boys drive her car too. So of course everyone wanted to come to my house because she was offering up her car and me! I drove as well. I figured since everyone else was driving, why not? She was also dangerous, so I felt it was safer if I drove. She hated to drive anyways and got into several accidents so I drove us everywhere. At this point, Jerry claimed me as his own property. He tried to beat up everyone and anyone that came near me. He wore me down, and I feel like he brainwashed me into believing he was the only one who loved me. My thoughts were now blurred and twisted.

I remember one time my mother wanted to go for ice cream so she told Jerry to drive us there. Of course I did not want to go, but I was forced to. As Jerry was flying through the parking lot weaving in and out of cars like a crazy man, my mother was laughing hysterically! I was yelling from the back seat to stop, but they both ignored me. Well, Jerry almost hit a woman as he pulled into a parking space. As we got out of the car the woman and her friends started screaming at him.

In an instant, Jerry just snapped and went crazy! He pulled out his pocketknife and started charging towards them. The women were looking at him in horror as he made his way around the car! My mom jumped in front of him to try to stop him, and he ended up stabbing her in the hand. Blood was squirting everywhere. I was blown away at what

I was witnessing. He was screaming bloody murder at them, as my mom was holding him back.

Somebody yelled, "Call the police!!!"

My mom screamed, "Get back in the car now, let's get out of here."

We did what she said, and got into the car, and he sped away. My heart was beating a mile a minute right out of my chest as we hopped into the car! People were all coming around as we sped off. I watched them yelling and pointing, but we were gone in a flash. I think he drove 100 miles an hour all the way back home, with my mom bleeding in the front seat. We got back into the house and they were both talking a mile a minute about what just happened and how much fun it was. I was completely sickened by the sight of both of them, as they were reenacting the scene over and over again. They were being so animated making faces and jumping up and down. As they proceeded to take their freak show outside to smoke together I retreated to my room and slammed the door!

Jerry continued to call me constantly and was always at our home. He even climbed in my bedroom window one night and tried to sleep in my bed with me. I told him to leave. My parents were in the next room sleeping. Another night he came to my window banging on it to let him in. I refused, and this time my dad heard him, and chased him through the yard. I was so happy that my father went after him, hoping to scare him away for good, but that was not the case at all.

He also went to NY with his mother and called me collect. I accepted, and didn't realize what that meant. He talked to me on the phone during the night for like two hours. He wanted to know everything that I was doing, and he was harassing me over and over again about other boys! No matter what I said to him, he told me I was a lying whore! When the phone bill came in my dad flipped out. He told me never to see him or talk to him again that he was a bad person. I just stared at him and he turned to my mother to show her the bill. She looked at him and said,

"Pay it you mother fucker and shut up!" He went ballistic!!! Another memorable moment at the Sega house hold!!

My dad hated him, and the more my dad hated him the more I clung to him because I was so angry with my dad for not being there for me. I was angry with him for leaving me with my mom, as he was off doing his own thing. I knew Jerry was bad, and I truly didn't want to be with him, but it was like he just took control of my brain, I couldn't think for myself anymore. He truly took over, like he said when he came into our home. He would tell me he would kill my whole family if I stopped talking to him. He told me my brother sent him to be with me. He also told me he was the devil and had powers to hurt me, and would hunt me down where ever I went. I was scared of him. I was powerless against his words… I was 12 and in 7th grade.

The last straw of my parent's marriage

The three of us went to the wedding of the youngest son of the owner of the bar we used to go to. My dad was in the wedding. He was also at that time having an affair with Kerry, the owner's daughter, who pretended to be friends with my mother. She even invited us over to her home, as she banged my dad!! I was aware of this. I knew she wanted my dad, I saw it at the bar all the time.

The wedding was a nightmare. My dad was drunk and my mom was crying, as she started to figure out about Kerry. There were words, many words. I went to the pay phone and called Jerry. My dad found me on the pay phone. "Lisa, who are you talking to?" I wanted to lie but I couldn't so I said Jerry. He ripped the phone out of my hand screamed at Jerry, "I will kill you if you ever set foot near my daughter again!" Then he threw the phone and dragged me out of the reception by my hair with my mother in tow. He threw me in the car, and he was screaming and driving like a mad man the whole way home. "Motherfucker, I will kill him. Joann, you're a fucking idiot for letting him in our house. I told you not to do it. You never listen to me. You are a crazy bitch. I hate you!" He pulled up in front of our house, dumped us off on the curb, and sped away. I was devastated. My mother was livid. We both stood there for a moment then we went inside…

My dad showed up at 5 a.m. and told my mother the marriage was over. He packed his stuff and left. He never said good-bye to me. I heard them talking as I lay in my bed crying like a baby. I knew at that moment my life was going to get even worse. This is when the severe torment began…

SILENT TEARS

A river of tears I cannot cry...
Hiding, cascading down the internal
Walls of my personal hell...

Inside my mind, pictures flashing so
Fast, I cannot keep the pace, one by one
In front of my face... The past a cold
Dark place to be, looking for the light to
Set me free...

A stone cold look flows across my face,

Anger
Hurt
Frustration

How am I to rate how deep into my
Soul this heartache burns, flipping then
Turns into a boiling pot of stagnant
Emotional waters ready to burst...

This boiling pot hit full steam ahead,
Rising so high, pressure building...

TIME IS UP!!!!

The explosion hits
With a fury, so damaging this
Natural disaster upon us...

Walls explode, dam broken, oceans of
Tears flowing out into the sea of life
Not stopping until the cease of all life...
At this moment life stands still, no
Conception of time, feeling like I have
Lost my mind...

Looking for my footing to hold me down,
Trying desperately not to drown...

Fighting to make it to the top, catch
A wave to bring me to the place where
Oxygen meets earth and all is at peace.

Looking for the open calm waters called
Tranquility, full of beauty and dignity...

This special place I do seek, forever
Searching digging in deep into this
Secret place called my heart forever
Broken torn apart...

CHAPTER 5

The Beast Within

Chapter 5

The Beast Within

My dad is now gone. I do get to see him at the bar and at my grandmother's house.

He is now living at my Aunt Cathy's house and dating Karen. He moved on with his life, and I was certainly not included. If I wanted to see him I had to go to the bar, or go to my grandmother's house to visit him. He did pick me up at times, but I was so angry with him I didn't even want to go. I was living at home with my mom who decided to stop taking her medications after he left. She was totally manic and crazy. She has a job (which to this day I do not know how she handled it.)

Jerry was now king of the household, and in total control. He thought he was on top of the world. When I think back to that time in my life I realize how much I hated him, I loathed him, but at the same time I listened to every word he said. If I would get defiant against him, he would beat me, and severely torment me. The psychological abuse alone was so profound, I was all screwed up. I was lost.

Now add in my mom's physical and emotional abuse on a daily basis, plus the anger and resentment towards my dad for leaving me to be abused this way—it was unbearable. I do not know how I survived this horrible year and a half of my life.

I felt so alone, and did not know how to handle it. I was a kid, a very screwed up, scared, and lonely kid, with no place to go, and nowhere to turn. I know family members knew what was going on, but not one person in my world jumped in to save me. That is not an exaggeration. That statement is the horrible truth. That memory has stayed with me to this day. NOBODY HELPED…. I have dealt with that anger and resentment for years, and it has taken a lot for me to overcome that anger and disgust.

Well, at this stage of my life the rapes had begun. Jerry would rape me all the time, taking what he claimed was his from day one. I was powerless, and I felt dirty and ashamed all the time. I would lie there and let him just do what he needed to do, and prayed to God it would be over quick. Sometimes it was not just about the sex, he liked to torment me, and say evil things to me.

I remember the first time he attacked me I was at my house, my mom was in the other room, sitting on the couch listening to music, crying, smoking, and talking to herself, and then it happened, he took his moment threw me to the floor and went for the full attack. I was in shock. I could not believe this is how my first sexual experience would be, and I was still so immature on that level, I wasn't even sure what was happening at first. Then it hit me, he was inside of me, raping me, choking me, hitting me, and laughing as he pumped harder and harder until he was done. I was sick, I cried, I was bleeding… Think about that, all this horror going on in one room, and my mom in the next totally oblivious of what was happening…or was she aware and just didn't care???

I often wondered that, because I felt she knew and did nothing about it. He would repeatedly take me in my spare room, my old play room and do whatever he felt he wanted to, and she just sat and smoked and smoked and smoked, cried and talked, and I was continually attacked, broken down, beaten, and alone, I was so lost… this went on for a year…

Some of the attacks were so crazy. One time he took me into the woods. He had a noose hanging on a tree, and he told me that it was for me. Secretly I thought *oh good, and then it will be over all the abuse will be over.* I would be with my brother and all these evil people could not touch me anymore, but that was not the case, reality set in when he hit me in the side of the head with a rock and proceeded to rape me right there as I lay on the ground. I watched the noose swing in the wind, and just cried. The more I cried, the harder he would pump, saying the devil was now inside of me releasing his cum into me wanting me to be pregnant with an evil child. He talked of how my brother said it was ok for him to take me this way. He said so many horrible things to me. He said I was his forever and he would do whatever he wanted and he loved the feeling of me being in pain. It empowered him. He would shout all these crazy verses of sick stories as he abused me. He took as much pleasure in beating me as he did in raping me. When it was over he would always tell me he loved me and I was his one and only and he was molding me to be his evil bride bound together forever. He was the sickest individual that I have ever met! Who says and does these kinds of things?

Another time he pulled me into the woods and forced me to perform oral sex on him. He jammed himself down my throat so hard. He held my head and I could not breathe. I was choking and he came down my throat forcing me to swallow every last drop, enjoying the thought of choking me with his cum. I was sick. When it was over I dropped to the ground and he kicked me so hard in the stomach twice, I began throwing up. He was enraged that I threw up his cum and was picking up the throw up and forcing it back into my mouth, dirt and all, forcing me to swallow it, holding my mouth shut until I did. I was so so sick… I wanted to die…

I felt like I was on the path to death. I remember one day he took me up to the lake to hang out with some people he knew. They were all older than me, much older! We were all sitting on the little beach area, as it was a very warm and sunny day. I remember feeling out of place and uncomfortable. They were all smoking pot, and acting strange. There was a lot of whispering, and they were staring at me. Jerry joined in, but I just sat silently wanting to leave. Everyone decided to go swimming. There was an old water pump station out in the lake, so we all swam out to it. It was about 15 to 20 feet from shore. It was all cement and a tube went straight up through the middle. One of the guys that were there told us that if you swim about 8 feet down there was a tube that went straight through to the other side. It was about 6 feet long. He bragged about how he had swum through that tube many times. Everyone was impressed. Jerry turned to me and said, "You have to swim through that tube!" I looked at him and said, "Why?" He wanted me to swim through it to prove to these nobodies that he had total control over me, and I would listen to anything he said. He started to berate me, and taunt me. He was loud and verbally abusive, and everyone laughed at me. I became angry and outraged. I felt like I might as well do it. Maybe I would get stuck down there, and die. Then it would be over. I seemed to have no regard for my life, as it was not my own anymore. I took the dare, and agreed to do it. I wasn't even scared. I jumped into the black water and swam down feeling my way along the wall. I found the tube. I looked up at the last bit of sunlight shining through the murky water, and went in. Once in the tube, I started to think about what was down there with me, and I got a little freaked out. I kept on talking to myself, and said, *stay calm Lisa, and keep on going.* I was half way through when I could see the light from the tube that stuck out of the top. I looked up into it, and the water in there was swaying slowly and I was mesmerized for a few moments. I then continued on until I finally made it out of the other side. I swam to the top, and sprung out of the water. I felt so proud of myself, and could not wait to rub it in Jerry's face that I did it, but everyone was gone! They all left me there, and swam back to shore. I stood on top of the water station, and looked towards shore. They were all packing up to leave, and Jerry was pointing and laughing at me. This infuriated me even further. What if I actually did not come out? I could have been stuck down there, and they didn't care! I swam to shore, and walked up to Jerry, and started to cuss him out. He hauled off and slapped me right across the face in front of the last couple of guys that were still there. He turned to them, and said watch this, and hit me again! Then he threw me to the ground ripped off my shorts and sexually assaulted me right in front of them. They seemed to be turned on at first, and then just turned and walked away. As they were leaving one of the guys yelled, "Have fun, you two!" I thought to myself, *I hope you both die!*

Then there was the time he brought me to his house and took me upstairs. His mother was downstairs with his sister, along with his two year old niece. His niece came upstairs and he brought her in the room, shut the door, and proceeded to rape me right in front of her. I remember her standing there just watching him attack me. I was mortified. I am thinking how could this poor child have to witness such a horrible sight? Then I thought what is she thinking. She came over to the side of the bed to get a closer look, and he talked to her while he continued to rape me, loving the fact that she was watching. He touched her as he hurt me. I told him to leave her alone and he punched me in the face and told me to shut up and enjoy it. When it was over he climbed off of me and picked her up and cuddled her touching her all over. Then he brought her back down to her mother. I wondered if he raped her too? It would not surprise me, as he seemed to take great pleasure in touching her. This incident was one of the most horrible things I had ever seen or been a part of, and thought I would rather him rape me than touch a baby…

Things for me just got continually worse. Day in and day out countless acts of abuse were preformed on me and I was trapped. I did not tell a soul. I just endured it hoping and praying one day it would be over one way or another. I can go on and on about what was done to me, but that would be like putting the CD player on repeat.

I can say this, with each and every moment of abuse, it made me feel dirtier, darker, and zombie-like. I was going through my days numb to the world around me. *How could no one see this?* I would think to myself sometimes. *I do not even know who I am anymore. I am lost, alone feeling dead inside, and at the same time my insides are screaming for help so deafening that I cannot think. Why can't anyone see this happening to me?* Everyone close to us at this point knew my mom was totally incompetent. They knew Jerry was at our house every day, and then, there were the visible bruises that I had. Why would everyone turn a blind eye to the nightmare I was living? Was I that worthless to the world? Unimportant and non-existent?

Those were the thoughts that would scream through my brain day in and day out. This negative dark force placed inside my soul was so loud I would want to smash myself in the head with a rock and end the torment. One day I woke up and hit my breaking point. I just had enough. I could not take another moment of this existence, so decided I would just end it myself.

HERE WERE MY THOUGHTS…

I would go up to the lake near my house and jump off at the waterfall, hit the rocks and it will be done and over with! I thought about it for a little while, and the thought of not suffering anymore sounded so wonderful and peaceful to me. The thought of my brother waiting for me was so inviting. He would take my hand and lead me home to a place where nobody could ever reach me, a place were I would truly be safe.

I was then on a mission. My mindset was focused on ending it all. I left the house and go. I do not remember my walk up to the lake, that was foggy and distorted, but I am now standing there at the top of this wall with all these thoughts going through my head, and the tears start flowing. I am this skinny little girl with big blue sad eyes wanting to end it all, but funny thing standing there alone in that moment I felt like someone or something was saying NO WAIT STOP. This is not the answer, don't do it. I heard these words loud and clear! ECHOING OVER AND OVER!!!! Everything then seemed fuzzy, and in slow motion like I was floating in a bubble. Imagine the silence in that bubble for a moment floating endlessly with a seemingly steady hum, like a bee buzzing along, hmmmmm bzzzzzzzzzz ohmmm. Twisting and turning over and over everything blurred, then POP!!!!

All of a sudden there was my mom standing at the bottom of the falls near the road screaming at me to get down at once. She had her cigarette in hand, crazy eyes, and hair teased up on end. Dressed in her classic tube top and shorts with her big clunky high-heeled shoes, with that bold red lipstick glaring in the sun. Watching her mouth move was like watching a 3-D movie, those red lips coming at me louder and louder. What a sight she was, and I was like what the hell, how did she know I was here, and what I was doing?

She kept on screaming, "Don't jump get down right now, do you hear me!" Ohh, I did hear her loud and clear, so I came down, baffled at the thought of her being aware enough in that moment to know what I was going to do. She has been in a world of her own for so long, and here was a moment of clarity at the last seconds when I wanted to end my life? I was more confused then ever. As I walked towards her she was ranting and raving like a lunatic, hands waving in the air. She grabbed me by the arm, squeezing me so tight and literally dragging me along as we walked home. She continued to yell at me for being stupid, foolish, and any other name she could think of. Once we hit the steps of the house, there was instant silence, like someone flipped a switch. It was like she went back into mechanical mode, and that glazed over look came back on her face. Her eyes were DEAD. You can only imagine what I was thinking. OK, all that yelling making a scene, and then silence once again. Madness, pure madness! It was never discussed again, and along came Jerry. Another horrible day finished out.

I was desperate to be noticed so one night I decided to run away. My mom went to sleep, and I left with my dog in tow. I walked down to a park near my home and slept under this huge pine tree with branches all the way to the ground. I climbed in along with my dog and had the best night sleep that I had in months. I felt comforted by the smell of the pine and the branches wrapped around me, and for once feeling protected. I loved listening to the wind blow in the cool night air, with the branches crackling in the dark echoing for all to hear. As I lay under that tree with my dog I imagined we were on a great journey looking for a new life. I was fantasizing about the tree rocking me and singing me sweet lullabies until I closed my eyes. In this fantasy world I am safe and warm, falling asleep with a smile. I woke the next morning, and of course I had nowhere to go, so I went home. I walked in the door and my mother had not even a clue that I was gone. I shouldn't have been surprised as she was in her own wicked little world oblivious to all around her. I was like OK… She never even noticed. She thought I got up early to walk the dog. I really am invisible, nobody even notices I am gone, especially my mother. She was the one who was supposed to be caring for me the most, but the truth is she was the one caring for me the least. I just lost it went to my room and cried my eyes out like I always ended up doing. Same scenario, I ran and cried and she mocked me. As I hit the door of my room I could hear her singing in the kitchen, "Mona Lisa, Mona Lisa!"

☙ THE BEAST WITHIN ❧

Trouble inside my head so deep, this insidious
Beast, self-destruction continually creeps,
As this beast never sleeps...

Slipping deeper into despair, wishing someone truly
Cared! Who will fight this beast? Chain reaction internal
Defeat, I fall to pieces once again, run in circles count to 10!

Then the explosion erupts, hits the street of personal
Hell, cobble stone beats - imprinted on sections of my
Heart a path to heartache from the start.

This emotional journey I am embarking on, battered and
Windblown personal scars...

Walls built up so high can the beast climb them hit the
Sky? Need to chase him out of my head, stop the
Noises, better off dead!!!!

Why do I need to fight, shield of Armor, my personal
Knight... Save myself from mass destruction, rebuild my
World, full of construction, replace the broken blocks with
Positive production...

Smashing the evil demon of the night, send him on a Final flight...

Beast be gone, I do say, pack your bags go Far away...

Peace in my mind is what I seek, permanent scars, Victory complete!

Medal of honor etched in my heart, survived the
Battle, my purple heart!

CHAPTER 6
Chaos

Chapter 6

Chaos

Over the next few months a lot went on. My parents did get divorced, and my mom was working but totally dysfunctional. It was at this time that I had to step up, and start grocery shopping and writing out bills. (I was 13 yrs old, and in the 8th grade.) I was going to school, being abused, and taking over a crumbling household. I drove regularly, as my mom did not like to drive anymore. The only place she would drive was to work and back. To this day I really do not know how she held a job at all. I know I have repeated that, but it is a thought that has never left me.

We had very little money so our phone got disconnected. This was another detachment from the outside world. Our electricity was turned off periodically as well. I think the worst was when we ran out of oil in the middle of winter. This day will stay with me forever burned in my brain. First the house was so cold you could see your breath. We had no money until the end of the week to order oil.

My dad couldn't have cared less. My mom told him, and he did not even do anything about it. His response was, "Figure it out." My mom sat at the table crying. At that moment I felt pity for her, as she was so alone herself lost in her own psychotic world drowning in her twisted thoughts. To make matters worse along came Jerry making his way in the house like King Tut, prancing in and deciding he was going to sleep over. I was like NO NO!!! My mom said, "Sure, we need to figure out a way to stay warm." His suggestion was to all sleep on the living room floor together. He ordered me to get blankets and pillows. I did as he said so I would not get beat up. I was tired and could not even fight anymore. I cooked us dinner, cleaned up, and it was time for bed, as he put it. My mom lay down, he lay in the middle, and I was on the other side. I was lying there feeling awful, so uncomfortable and awkward. I was stiff as a board praying he would not touch me.

I thought he fell asleep because he was quiet, and then it started. He was putting his hands all over me. I was lying there thinking if I ignore him, maybe he will stop. NO chance. He pulled my pants down and from behind forced his way inside me. I was frozen in fear, and sick to my stomach. My mom was lying right there. He pushed his way in as he always did. I was defenseless. He pumped away until he was done, even moaning. It was finally over and he fell asleep. I just cried and lay there until the sun came up. My mom got up and so did Jerry. Another day began. I had to get ready and go to school, and of course he came with me. How could this be happening to me? What did I do in life to deserve this disgraceful treatment? I used to ask myself that question all the time. I would make my way to school and try to forget what was going on.

I remember sitting in class and my mind started to wander. How could my mom not know what happened to me last night, or ever! How could she be lying right next to us and not know? I get home from school and my mother was sitting there at the table. I walked in, and she said to me, was I dreaming last night or was Jerry having sex with you? He was moving around a lot. I looked at her, and was like what the fuck! I said, "What do you think happened last night?" She said I don't know, but it sounded good! I think that had to be one of the most repulsive things my mom had ever said to me, and I could not even respond. I walked away, went to my room, sat on my bed, and just rocked for a long long time. What kind of monster was she to say that, not care, and even think it was exciting? I felt so low, nasty scum like dirt on someone's shoe. I could not get any lower. At that moment I just gave up. I didn't care about anything anymore. I was a dead carcass of a young girl just going through the motions of hell on earth.

I would go to school and he would be there. I would look out my classroom door and he would be standing there staring at me. There was no escape from him. One day we were standing in line in the lunchroom. There was this quiet boy standing behind us. Jerry was giving me a hard time, for whatever reason I cannot remember. He said to me because of you, now I have to beat up this kid behind us in line. I begged him not to hurt that boy who was so meek. Jerry didn't care, and he pounced. He grabbed this kid; I remember the fear in his eyes! I watched in horror as he beat the shit out of him for no reason. The fight was finally broken up, and Jerry was screaming all these crazy devil—worshiping verses, and pointing at me shouting, see what you made me do, it's all your fault. I just cried and ran from the cafeteria. This was the first day I ever skipped school. I ran outside and ran as fast as I can. I ran all the way home, which was quite far away. I got to my house and locked myself in, fearing he would come for me. I hid in my closet for hours until my mom finally came home. As usual she was clueless.

Of course, Jerry was suspended, and I had a reprieve at school. I found a little bit of peace and happiness there for this very short period of time. I could learn, which is what I wanted to do. Talk to people and not feel like he was glaring at me every moment. Enjoy my art class, which was my favorite, and I was quite good. Then my reprieve was over, and he was back to pick up where he left off. He told me there was a girl name Ada who wanted him, and he instructed me to beat her up. I did not want to beat her up, or anyone else for that matter. I was not a violent person. He told me that if I did not do as he asked then the beating I would take would be the worst one yet. He told this girl to meet me on the green after school and we would fight for him! Could you imagine this pompous ass, thinking he was worth anyone fighting over him, this low life individual. He brought me to the green after school. There were like 50 kids there as the rumor went through the school. This was 8th grade and you know how kids at that age are, they cannot pass up on a good fight, especially a chick fight.

We were standing there, and she started saying things to me. Well at that moment I unleashed all my anger and aggression onto her. The poor girl never saw it coming. I beat the fuck out of her like I never imagined that I could. Everyone was chanting, and I just kept on swinging. I hated every blow I gave to her, but at the same time I was fighting for my life. I was letting out all my held in hostility toward my life, Jerry, my mom, my dad, and my family who had left me there to rot in hell. These were the images that flashed before my eyes with every blow, like a silent movie. It seemed like it went on forever. Blood was everywhere. I beat her face so bad, and then all of a sudden I felt someone grab me and pick me up off of her. I was like 85 pounds, this skinny little thing full of rage. This woman grabbed me turned me around and started shaking me, screaming in my face, "What are you doing?" over and over again. I looked at her everything was slow and distorted my head was spinning. I looked directly into her eyes, and I pulled away and I ran as fast as I could. I was crying, and right behind me was Jerry chasing me. I ran but he caught me. He stopped me, and was like you didn't finish the job. He slapped me across the face right on the side of the road. Then he slapped me again, and I fell to the ground, feeling the sting across my cheek. Tears welled in my eyes, as he stood over me and laughed. He was saying all this stuff to me, about being a coward and weak. He told me I was useless, and need to learn how to follow his commands. He pulled me to my feet, and dragged me to my house. I tried to pull away, but every time I did his grip became harder and stronger. It was like a clamp with no release in site. I knew once we made our way through the door I was in serious trouble. The fear inside me grew as he dragged me home, a place that was supposed to be my safe haven from all evil; which was now his playground. Once inside I took the beating of my life, and the worst experience of rape one could endure. He stuck things in every part of me, until I was bleeding and he went on for what seemed like forever. When it was finally over, he got up and left. I dragged myself to the shower and blood poured out from my rectum where he used a pocketknife to carve away at my insides. What a nightmare I was living! I was broken on every level possible. I was this frail little girl, beaten and bleeding, trying to shower off all the shame and embarrassment. I scrubbed and scrubbed for what seemed like an eternity, but it did not cure me. I was poisoned by the harsh truth of my life bestowed upon me. Damaged beyond repair by the smell of rape and torture. The residue of mental illness stained my body and my being forever branding me with the curse of my mother.

Later my mother finally came home oblivious to anything that happened earlier in the day. If the walls could talk they would tell a sick tale of abuse and horror. If the walls could talk she would not have listened anyways. The only voices she heard were the ones in her brain controlling every move she made. Commanding her to do bad things and torture everyone who set foot in her path. Her wicked tongue that can cut you like a knife in a moment, and chop you up leaving you for dead. This is mental illness at its worst, but in her thought process she was at her best.

That horrible day was finally over, and I went to bed. I lay there and thought about all the wrongs that were done to me. I think of my brother, and why he left me alone. I think, *how much more am I supposed to take?* I pray and fall asleep. The next day I get up, pull myself together and start a new day praying for a different outcome…

☙ CHAOS ❧

Chaos all around, trying to run from the sound...

Nowhere to hide, feeling out of control, hate being
Told what to do, what to say, wanting it to go all
My way...

How can I stay up in here, sound so deafening,
I just can't hear...

Wanting my peace and serenity a feat seeming
Unable to greet!

What can I say," Please leave me alone, go away!"

Looking for my serenity, the peace
I deserve, a place to be me.

See me sitting all alone? Gain composure, another
Stepping-stone.

Finding my way through the pain, figuring it out
Stopping the rain.

Let the voices go away, noise ending, no more pain.

I wake this morning no crazy display, stepping it up, I
Have made my way.

Thank you Lord for my brand new day!

BREAK
THE
CHAINS

CHAPTER 7
Whatever May Come

Chapter 7

Whatever May Come

After that beating something inside of me started to change. I felt myself changing. I wanted change! I needed change!

My thoughts were everywhere—so clouded, but surreal at the same time. I kept thinking, "I need to get myself out of this situation!" He told me I was weak and nothing for so long I totally believed him. I truly felt worthless to the world. My silent cries for help went unnoticed. Then I started to process all of this on a different level. All the wrongs that were being done to me! Why ME??? If no one had come to my rescue at that point, then they never would. Not my mom—she was lost in her own fucked-up world of misery and pain. Not my dad who was desperately searching for a new life, leaving my mother and me behind. Then there was my family. You have to love them! (Oh yes, the sarcasm.) We were all supposed to be so close, but they had a blind eye to all of it. I felt so betrayed. I felt like the family that I thought I knew was one big lie. I know they knew what was going on, which made it more painful to think about. My grandmother who was blind even knew what was up, and she would send my grandfather to check in on us, and send food, but that was the extent of any outside help— a blind woman and a drunk. Family members would briefly come and go, preach to my mother and me, and then leave. People were talking, but nobody was listening. Nobody chose to see the reality of what was really going on in this house of horrors.

I accepted the realization that I was on my own. I was a 13-year old girl with all this chaos going on in my world, and I was the only one who could save myself. That was one big feat for this little girl. I remember staring in the mirror looking at myself. I was small and skinny. I hardly ever ate. My eyes were as blue as the sky, and my long dark brown hair flowed down my back. I looked pale and sullen. I was thinking where am I? Where did I go? Am I actually still in there? I started touching my face, and then pinching my arms, barely feeling it lost in the thoughts inside my mind. This was the first time in a very long time that I started to think of what I wanted in the future. What did I want? What did I deserve? I certainly deserved better than this, and I kept on saying it to myself over and over again. I even wrote it in my notebook over and over like 1000 times. I would read it out loud to encourage myself to be strong. In the darkness of the night when I was alone, I would pull out my book and study those words, talking to myself, praying for change.

I promised myself that very day that someday it would all change, and I would break free of all of the abuse. At that point in my life, I had not told a soul what was going on. I would go to school and pretend everything was fine. Can you imagine being out and about acting like everything was ok? (Oh everyone knew my mother was crazy as she did the most outrageous things. I will dedicate a special set of writings to my mom and her behavior. That alone is a long and winding story of mania and terror. That is one story I have never dared to write about, but I am ready to do so now!) I was known as the girl whose brother died, and whose mom went crazy. Yes, that was my title all through school. Everyone knew of my dad as a loud crazy Italian man who made his presence know to all. Yes, that was me, with that title sitting heavy on my shoulders, but nobody truly knew the reality of it all! I was really good at hiding it, holding it all in. I perfected it. You could say I was a mastermind.

I went on through my days trying to hold it together the best that I could. My mom was getting worse, and was not able to hold it together at work anymore. Everyone at work despised her because of her behaviors. She was eventually fired from her job, but she managed to get another one for a short period of time.

Jerry was still coming and claiming what he thought was his, but I was changing towards him and he knew it. He could see it in me as I was becoming more defiant with him and foul mouthed. I refused to be silent, and took every opportunity to be nasty towards him. Don't get me wrong, I took some good beatings for it, but I figured I was not going down without a fight. I would find ways not to be home so I didn't have to deal with him or my mother. I learned how to disappear, and keep them guessing. I started hanging out with a new group of kids. I was searching for other outcasts like me, who didn't ask questions, and I found them. I felt good when I had the upper hand on Jerry and my parents.

Jerry would try to track me down and I would hide from him. I became quite clever on outsmarting him, and he hated it. He was losing his control a little bit at a time, and I kept pushing. My biggest downfall was my mom; she always pushed him back onto me. She was relentless. At this point my dad started popping up a little bit more, and Jerry was scared of him so he would run every time my dad showed up. I remember one time my dad came in the house, and Jerry was hiding in the closet. My mom was yelling at my dad for just showing up. My dad was screaming at her that it was still his house and he would come any time he wished. My mother unleashed her foul mouth onto him and she was vicious. I stood there silent, and I kept on looking at my dad making eye contact, and then looked at the closet. He realized what I was doing, and went over to the closet and opened it. Jerry came popping out, and started running. The look on his face was priceless, pure terror as my dad reached for him! My dad went ballistic and chased after him. I got the biggest laugh of my life that day, as I watched my dad chase Jerry through the neighbors yard trying to catch him. I got a gift on that day as well—Jerry never came back, and neither did my dad. He got into his car screaming and swearing as he drove away. Of course when he left, my mother turned her anger onto me, and sliced me up with her switchblade of a tongue. In disgust, I went to my room and slammed the door and locked it. She proceeded to bang on it for a bit bellowing every swear word in her vocabulary, but then just gave up. I heard her in her room crying and swearing at God. I didn't come out for the rest of the night.

My dad's new mission was stalking Jerry, and trying to catch up with him to beat the shit out of him. He was waking up slightly to what was happening to me, but he was never consistent so things started getting really crazy. I was getting in trouble at school regularly, and skipping. I thought nothing of telling a teacher to go fuck himself or herself, and I beat up a couple of more girls. There was a girl named Suzie, who kept on talking about me, and telling everyone I was crazy because my brother died. This enraged me, as I knew I was not crazy, and who was she to even mention my brother! I caught up with her in the stairwell between classes, and I walked up to her and punched her square in the face like four times, before a teacher came to break it up. I was screaming at her as they were dragging me away. "That is what you get for talking about my brother! Who the fuck do you think you are even mentioning his name, I will kill you next time!!!!"

My anger was seeping out everywhere in my life. I could not contain it a moment longer. I was this out of control girl, with a wicked tongue just like my mother. The things I would say were horrible. I wanted to be noticed, and now I was, but for all the wrong reasons. I spent more time in the principal's office over the next couple of months than anyone

I knew. I had straight F's on my report card, and I was proud to present that report card to my father over dinner one evening. I loved the shock factor! He went ballistic as I expected he would. Then to rub salt in the wound I told him his girlfriend was a douchebag and a whore. The funny thing about that was she was sitting right there. Well, you can imagine the outcome of that whole dinner experience. She chased me around the table, and if she'd gotten a hold of me that night, she would have beaten the crap out of me. Who could blame her, because I was awful and mean. I was angry. When I look back on that moment, it's mind blowing. My dad yelling, Karen chasing me, and I was enjoying every minute of it. I was getting more negative attention. It was empowering. I took great pleasure in watching my dad freak out. My sweet revenge! Needless to say my dad drove me home to my mother. He dumped me off, screamed at my mom, and left. This was typical behavior for him. That is what he did, come in like a tornado, scream, and leave. I saw the back of his head so often it was not surprising, but it did cut like a knife every time he left. In my mind I was screaming please take me with you I will be good, just love me and keep me safe. That is all I really wanted, but I could not get the words out.

My anger just kept on growing, and I was now lashing out at my mom, and we would fight viciously. She would beat the crap out of me all the time. I didn't care; I kept pushing everyone's buttons, my mom, Jerry, my dad, the teachers, and anyone else who got in my way. When I think of my behavior it was vile! So now I am creating attention, and at that point you would think someone would step up and step in. Nope, sad to say, that would not be the case. My foul behavior was being chalked up to my parents divorcing, and me looking for their attention. This infuriated me even more, and gave me more motivation to act out. With all the controversy going on something had to give. It went on way too long, and my day finally came. It came in a way that I did not want or expect, but I was relieved. This is the day my mother tried to kill herself!

I woke up like every other day, went off to school, and my mom left for work. At this point Jerry was expelled from school, so when I was there it was my open playground to create any type of havoc I wanted. I felt I had free reign to do whatever I wanted, and proceeded to do so. When I got home that day Jerry was waiting for me on the steps. My stomach got an instant pit when I saw him. I thought to myself, *oh no what will happen today?* I was sickened by the site of him, and numb to what was going to happen to me. I learned how to separate and disassociate the feelings when he touched me and abused me. His words meant nothing to me now, and I would block his voice out of my head. He would be talking to me, and it would be a slow motion echo, distorted and dream-like. This is the only way I can describe how it sounded. It was crazy, but I know I was trying to protect myself any way possible, so if it was dream-like, it wasn't real. I know that sounds so warped when I say that, but it is funny what the brain will do to protect you from an abuser.

We went inside the house and of course he was right on me, forcing me into the bathroom. He wanted to shower with me and have his fun in there since my mother was not home yet! I was thinking there are not enough showers in the world to wash off the scum of his touch, just the essence of him was appalling. I did as he said. I undressed, got into the shower, and let him do his business, but on this day he did not just want the shower experience. When he was done in there he dragged my by my long hair to my bedroom and continued his garish attack on me. My window was open and at one point I saw my neighbor peering in watching us. I was thinking this old fuck is getting off on this, not even realizing I was being raped! When he realized I saw him he ran from his window and it continued until he was satisfied with himself, dropping every last ounce of his cum inside me telling me he wants me to have his baby. I was just sickened by the thought of it. Having his baby, please! At this point I was looking at the clock and wondering where my mother was. She was usually home by now and it was getting late. As I did not have a phone, I went to my other neighbor and asked to borrow her phone. I called my aunt Ro and asked her if she had heard from my mother. She said NO. I told her I was worried. It was around 5 p.m. My aunt called my dad. My aunt came to my house and told Jerry to leave as my dad was on the way. Of course he ran like a deer scared shitless, the fucking coward. My dad came and said he will go look for her. My aunt took me to my grandma Rose's house where I waited up all night for news. I was worried sick about her; all I wanted was my mother to come home safe. I was angry with her for the way she treated me, and what I was subjected too, but this was still my mom and I was afraid for her, I still loved her very much.

At 6 a.m. the next morning my mom came walking in the door. They found her in the woods near her work place. She had cut both her arms all the way down with a razor. She tried to kill herself. I ran up to her put my arms around her, and nothing! My mom wasn't there. She had the zombie-like look on her face that I'd seen years before when they came in and told me my brother passed away. I moved back away from her. I was like, "Mom I was so worried, are you all right? Please talk to me." There was silence. She walked right past me into the bathroom, and went and lay on the bed. I knew that silence. It was the silence before the storm. My mind started racing, my heart pounding in my ears. I knew once she was recharged, it was going to be bad.

I was so hurt by her response, but then again why did it shock me? It was what happened all the time. She was manic and it was either one extreme or the other. I guess as a kid you still have that inner hope that this time it will be different! I was no different than any other kid. I just wanted my mother to love me and take care of me.

My mom finally woke up, and to no surprise she was in full form. I knew her like a book. Her wicked tongue lashing out at everyone, even yelling out the front door to the neighbors across the street. What a vulgar display, and then the sexual content was off the chart. We tried our best to keep her under control. Imagine this scenario, my grandmother is blind, my grandfather is a drunk, and here I am just a kid going from one bad situation to the next. We did the best we could. When my mother was like that nobody could handle her. My dad came and picked me up the next morning. He told me I was going to go live with him and Karen for a while until my mom got better. My mother was seeing spaceships, and the blessed Mother Mary outside in the trees. She was hallucinating and totally lost from reality. I left that day, with her screaming out the door, and my grandfather holding her back. She was cursing my dad for stealing me, and told him she was calling the police. My dad looked at me and said sternly, "Get in the car, and do not look back!" My heart actually broke for her, as she stood there screaming, but I was so happy to be getting away from her. I felt guilty for leaving her, but I needed some peace. I needed a break from taking care of her.

My mom was eventually brought to the hospital to the psychiatric ward, a place that knew her all too well—a place I visited on several occasions and hated. I feared that place, the people, and their behaviors. It was like walking into a psychedelic haunted house—everything was animated and loud. As a child this is how I viewed it, and had terrible nightmares about it. I knew it was going to be bad for her, and she would fight tooth and nail with everyone there. I knew she would punch, scratch, kick, and bite. They would inject her with drugs and put her in restraints. She would be black and blue all over. I did not want to visit her, but I also knew at some point I would have to. The thought of seeing my mother like that always tore at my heartstrings. It devastated me to see her locked up and in so much pain, mentally and physically. I wanted to save her. I wanted to save me. I also wanted someone to save us!

On one hand I was feeling like my nightmare is over, as my dad pulled out of the driveway that day. I was finally out of that house, and I was with my dad. That was something I had deeply wanted for so long. I wanted his nurturing and attention. I felt he could protect me from all the bad things that were happening to me, and things would get better. So I thought.

WHATEVER MAY COME

Like blind vigilant soldiers we march on
Through time...

Never knowing what will be the new
Rhyme.

Thoughts of bright futures lay ahead, no
Thoughts of tragedy one could dread...

Meticulously we plan every move, hoping
It all will come true... Never knowing

What twist or turn life may take, contemplating
Our next mistake...

Forever the optimist I will be, not
Wanting to deal with misery... Like the
Strong soldier that I am, always ready to
Take a stand!

With my strong faith to lead the way, I will make
It through every passing day...

With this faith I profess, I will make it, pass the
Test...

Whatever may come, bring it on, I will be
Prepared fully armed...

This blind soldier I will be, fighting for
My dignity...

Full of love and pride, having
My angel by my side; leading this soldier
Through ever-lasting time...

CHAPTER 8
Little Girl Lost

Chapter 8

Little Girl Lost

Short time living with my Dad!

My dad lives in an apartment with his girlfriend Karen. It is a one bedroom, so I am forced to sleep on the couch. I am angry with my dad for leaving me behind, and feeling that he has chosen a new girl and a new life before me. This is the resentment I had towards him. Now, add in all the rest of the crap I went through; needless to say I was an extremely angry young girl. My father did not have a clue about just how angry I was, but he will figure it out! He just didn't see it coming.

My mom is in the hospital now, and I am forced to talk to her on the phone when she calls. She sounded crazier then ever. She is singing and cursing on the phone, and I did not even want to deal with her. At times she would talk so fast that I could not even understand her. This was mania at its peak with the hysterical laughing, and she is spitting and urinating on herself. She is basking in the psychotic freedom that she is embracing like a new lease in life. She is demanding her cigarettes, and telling me she is having sex with all the men in the hospital and loving it. She stated to me, "Lisa I am going to live here forever. I am having the time of my life with these pricks." She goes on to say that she spoke with my aunt and said she can screw up a wet dream. I am appalled by her voice. I cannot even believe this is my mother! Why does she have to be MY mother?

I am now finishing out 8th grade. It is almost Summer now.

My dad is gone most of the time, and so is Karen. I am home alone a lot. If they were not working, they were down at the bar. They lived a fast-paced lifestyle that was wild and crazy. The bar was their main focal point. I would sometimes go down there and sit at the bar with them; my dad would make me a screwdriver or White Russian. I would drink my drink and look around soaking up all the activity transpiring in front of me. Not normal, right? Well, my family was anything but normal.

My dad took a stand, and instructed me not to see Jerry anymore. It was strange how I felt about that. You would think I would be like great, I am done with that horrible situation, but there was still a weakness inside of me drawing me back to him. Maybe it was my dad saying not to do it! I was angry and untrusting of him. I mean Jerry told me for almost two years that my dad didn't love or care about me. I felt he proved it by leaving me there with my mother, and moving on without me. My head was so screwed up, and I could not make any clear decisions. I felt so weak and vulnerable. I had nobody to talk to who would even remotely understand how I was feeling. How could I explain what has happened to me, and make is sound normal or ok? I was filled with embarrassment and shame; anger and regret for not being stronger. I felt like dirt stuck under someone shoe. Bottom line I felt alone.

Once in a while Jerry would show up and want to talk to me. I would actually talk to him. Why I am totally not sure. Was it some type of withdrawal from the abuse? Was it to get my dad back? I honestly think it was a little bit of both. When I think back to this time in my life, I am sad because I seem so weak. It makes me quite upset even to this day to think of myself in that light. This is not the type of person that I ever wanted to be, but when someone is continually abused they lose the ability to think and feel beyond the abuse. The hardest part of abuse is breaking the cycle. That is what I needed to learn how to do, break the cycle forever.

Summer came, and my dad and Karen were partying up a storm and fighting a lot. He is a force to be reckoned with, and then add the alcohol. He was a manic. She was no better—they were like oil and water when they were drunk, and the fighting was vicious. I remember one night at the bar they got into a huge fight. We were all there drinking, and my dad just flipped out and left. He had a jealousy streak that was a mile long, and a short fuse. He screamed and ranted, and then took off in his car. Karen took me and we chased after him in her car. She caught up to him and they were both doing like 90 miles an hour on the stretch of road by the beach. It was so scary. Karen was crying and yelling as she drove like a mad woman after him. We suddenly came to this sharp corner, and the car that we were in started tipping. We were on two wheels turning that corner! It happened so fast. We were both screaming and yelling. The car was tipping and our lives hung in the balance.

This was such typical behavior for my dad when he was in a drunken rage. He drove like a manic, and had no regard for human life, his or anyone else who happened to be with him. I had been in the car with him on several occasions when he would do over a 100 miles an hour raging like a caged animal! We were lucky never to crash. Karen and I were also blessed that night to make it around that corner and live to tell about it. I felt there was always an angel with us; I do believe it was my brother.

That night we almost crashed, Karen and I. After she regained control of the car, we went home. She was so frightened. She kept on saying, "What am I doing, I could have killed you! Your father is crazy!" I didn't say anything, but I knew she was right. Both of my parents were crazy people, and there was not a thing I could do about it. We were emotionally wiped out and both went to bed. My dad showed up hours later, and woke up Karen and starts fighting with her. He ended up pushing her, and he hit her right in the chest. I witnessed this and my natural reaction was to try to stop my dad. Deep inside I truly liked Karen, but at that time I would never admit to it. Well, stepping in was a bad mistake, as he grabbed me and threw me across the room, and I hit the wall. Karen hit him back, and grabbed me then we left running. Then we were driving again, and we were both crying. We decided to get a hotel room that night, as we had nowhere else to go. It was awful. I felt bad for her, and for me. We both lay there in bed that night, but neither one of us slept. We didn't talk either. The silence was eerie. The next morning we got up, had some breakfast and went back home like nothing had happened. This is a seriously dysfunctional pattern in my life, awful things would happen and everyone pretended all was ok.

Things just seemed so out of control on every level of my life, and here was Jerry in the background trying to pull me back. He still had some kind of hold on me. I honestly do not know what compelled me to see him alone the next day. Was it force of habit? Was it the mind games he would play with me? I did not even want to see him, so why did I? When he showed up at the apartment complex I was disgusted by the sight of him. He took me directly into the basement and proceeded to beat and rape me. During all of this, I was thinking what did I just do to myself! Why would I put myself in this position again, after I promised myself I would get out of this situation? Was I punishing myself for feeling like such a bad person? I was so disappointed in myself, and knew I was truly fucked up. This incident pushed me further into depression, with my self-esteem of negative zero.

I turned to drinking and smoking pot with my friends to try to numb the pain.

My friends were clueless to what was happening in my life, and when I was drunk or high none of it mattered. I felt like I was floating free above it all, and I felt like nothing could touch me. The summer keg parties were out of control, and being chased by police was exciting. I was really getting into the party scene. I fed off the excitement and my adrenaline would be rushing full steam ahead. I was wild and out of control, and it felt great! Thinking about it now makes me think of my mother in her moments of mania. You get addicted to the feeling and you do not want it to end. I can now understand my mother's need for that out of control feeling. It was empowering, like being a super hero. There are no boundaries, just freedom to be bad without consequence.

That summer Jerry got too cocky for his own good. He went to the bar where people knew my father and started bragging about how good I was and how he enjoyed knocking me around. He told everyone that I always came back for more!

He went on to tell people disgusting things about me, and how I would even have sex with him while I had my period. The blood was a turn on for him. I don't know why he would do that knowing my dad was a mad man. I guess he felt he was above it all as well. He must of thought he was untouchable. He was definitely too cocky!

Well, it didn't take long for my dad to get wind of this, and he was on the move again trying to track him down. I do believe he wanted to kill him dead. He screamed at me so bad, and blamed me for all of it. Our conversation consisted of every swear word you could imagine, and me just quivering. This gave me yet another reason to be defiant and angry. As I was quivering, I could feel myself burning inside. I wanted to just scream at top of my lungs, "Dad he raped me, he abused me over and over again, and where were you? I needed my father and you were not there!" This is what I wanted to say, but what I actually did was bow my head and just say, " I am sorry, Dad. I know I am a disappointment." I was defeated again, hopeless, and lost.

The misery continues...

Summer was now in full bloom; I was out as much as possible. I never ate anymore, and I was down to about 80 pounds. My dad and Karen had this love/hate relationship, and fought all the time. They also drank all the time, which didn't help. They were textbook dysfunctional.

It was so bad that I could predict what they would say to each other. As they fought, I would recite it all in my head word for word before they would actually say it. It was like a game for me, trying to get as many words right as I could. I assume this was another coping method I was teaching myself to dull the pain, and deal with the situation. They sounded so stupid, that I could not even believe they were adults. They were petty, foolish, and just obnoxious. I just wanted them to shut up! In my head I was screaming at top of my lungs, "Shut the fuck up!!" Sad part, in the morning they would get up and be all lovie dovie together like nothing ever happened. They would have coffee, chat, and go to work. I was always amazed how their demeanor went from one extreme to the other. Literally the phrase "Like Night and Day" fit them perfectly.

My mom finally got out of the hospital towards the end of summer, but my dad didn't want me to go back to her yet, as she was still having major issues. She was living at my grandparent's house and I would go visit her. It was always the same thing. She did her out of control antics, and crazy talk. I could recite her words as well; they were engraved in my mind. I just endured it, and then went back to my dad's house. I did stay away from Jerry, as I didn't want to go through that again. I was done with his abuse, and knew if I talked to him I would end up back in the basement. He would try to hunt me down, and my dad would try to hunt him down. It was one big crazy game, until one night when my dad finally caught up with him.

It was at the roller-skating rink that I would always go to. My dad was drunk and went in and found him. Jerry ran into the bathroom to hide in a stall. My dad went in and proceeded to kick the shit out of him, kicking him punching him, in a total rage. He was screaming and yelling obscenities as he knocked his front teeth out of his mouth. It took 6 police officers to pull him off of him, and off to jail he went. A lot of my friends were there to witness this gruesome display, and it was talked about for years. Everyone was terrified of my dad!

Karen came home that night and tells me my dad is in jail, and asked what happened. I was emotionless. I don't think I even really responded to it. Inside I felt like yes, he finally got the beating he deserved. I almost thought I would have loved to see his face cower like I used to every time I felt the sting of his hand across my face! Then I felt sadness, as I truly hated violence and my dad was out of control and scary. Then I felt bad my dad was in jail, I just wanted him home. I wanted a normal life some how, that was all I wanted was to be given a normal life. I sat and cried for all these reasons alone in my misery. Karen didn't say anything else to me; she seemed very angry with me like it was my entire fault.

My dad and Karen knew a lot of people in the police department, so the next morning my dad was released and they told him if Jerry dropped the charges against him they would let him go with no further actions. My father knew everyone, and had connections wherever he went. Some times he would walk into a place, and you would think a celebrity just walked in the door. He was catered to all the time. Big Bad John, he was larger than life, his essence was of total power and strength.

My dad and Karen came home and I did not want to face him, as I could only imagine what he was going to say to me. They came in, and sit me down. They told me that I had to go to Jerry and beg him to drop the charges. I could not believe what I was hearing. It was bad enough that my mom offered me up to this devil; now my dad was doing the same thing to save his own ass. Yes, offer up the piece of shit worthless little girl, it doesn't matter, that is all that was pounding through my brain as the words sunk in. I was like I do not want to see him. They said it was my fault my dad was in this mess and I needed to make it right. I should have just stayed away from him, and this would not be happening right now. My heart sunk like a brick. My protector, My savior, My dad just sold me down the river to save his own soul. I was silent once again. I told him I would go see him, and make it right.

The next day I went to the armory where Jerry worked, and found him. He was beaten up really bad, and I actually smiled when I saw him. They had to sew his teeth back in, he was a mess. He ranted about how my father beat him up, and I was to blame for his troubles. I told him I needed to talk with him about what happened. I pleaded for my dad, begged him like a dog not to have him go to jail. He took great pleasure listening to me beg. He smiled this wicked smile, and said you know you have to pay the price right? I just looked at him sickened by the thought of what would come next. He took me right there in the armory. Forced me to do all sorts of things to him. Making me beg for my dad through the whole thing. He would hit me and say, "Beg, bitch, beg! Who is in charge of you! You are worthless trash," and then he started chanting devil-worshiping phrases cursing my soul and my dad's, so empowered. He was so crazy with his eyes popping out of his head, with this twisted smirk. Then he shoved his cock down my throat once again forcing me to swallow every ounce of his cum laughing at me, mocking me for choking. He slapped me around for a while and then said he was through for now, but he will get me again. He said he would drop the charges, but when he wanted me he would find me and if I did not obey him then he would kill my father. I was back to square one. My dad sold me to the devil, and I was at his mercy.

He did as he said he dropped the charges, my dad was a free man, and I was doomed to rot in hell. Over the next couple of weeks he would show up at my apartment when nobody was there drag me down the basement and do his business. I was defenseless again. I could not believe this was happening to me again, but I was terrified he would kill my dad. I did everything he said.

Once again my dad found out he was coming around and blamed me for this. He told me to once again tell him we could not see each other anymore. I was like what do I do now? I am in a no-win situation. I cannot tell my dad the truth, as I could not get the words out as to how

I was feeling or what was happening to me. If I say anything to Jerry I truly felt he would have killed my dad he was that crazy. I was beside myself, with worry and fear. I really wanted to run away, far away where nobody could find me.

Summer was now over and school was starting again, and at the same time, my grandfather (my father's dad) was dying of cancer. Yes, in the middle of all this chaos my grandfather was very sick, and we would go visit with him a lot. I loved him very much. He was a good man, and was very good to me when I was a child. It was heartbreaking to watch him suffer, and wither away eaten up by cancer. I always felt like the good people were all being taken away from me in my life, and it was like I did not deserve them.

I did see Jerry a little bit longer, as I was too afraid to tell him what my dad said. I was now back in school, starting the 9th grade, and yearning for a normal existence. Once again I worked up the courage and I decided that I would tell Jerry he needed to go. I was so done with the abuse, and I would take the chance of him trying to do something to my family, as I was desperate to save myself. I needed to be strong and take back my life!

I prepared myself the best that I knew how, and went see him by the train tracks near my house. I told him what my dad said, and he went into a rage. I told him I was done, I could not do it anymore, and I tried to walk away. I thought if I did it quick that maybe I could get away. I was frightened, and I wanted to run. What a bad move I made, I turned my back on him. He grabbed me from behind smashed my head on the train tracks and brutally raped me right there. He kept hitting me, and pumping so hard, I thought he would go right through me. When it was over he told me that my family and me were all dead. I thought I am already dead so what does it matter. I got up collected myself, wiped off all the dirt from the ground and went home. This time when I left I backed away slowly, watching him as he sneered at me, face all twisted. He cursed me until I was out of sight, then I turned and ran as fast as I could all the way home. My heart pounding in my chest thinking he was on my heels. I turned around a few times, but he was nowhere in sight. I came in the door and my dad saw my bruises and I was bleeding. I told him Jerry hit me when I told him I would not see him anymore. I did not mention the rape. My father went into another fit of rage, and tried to find him, but Jerry went into hiding when he heard my dad was after him. I am sure the thought of another beating at the hands of my father would be too much for him. He was truly a coward. He knew how to dish it out, but he certainly could not take it.

I was just lost as this point, more lost then ever. My dad had disappointed me on such deep levels that I cannot even begin to express the feelings of that. My mom was totally out of it, and I felt totally betrayed by both of them. These were the people who brought me into this world. They were supposed to protect me always, and neither one did. I hated them both for letting this happen to me. I felt like this is not how my life was supposed to be. I wondered if my brother didn't die, would we all be together? My brother was gone, my parents were crazy, and I just wanted to start living my own life away from them both, but I couldn't. I was stuck.

Over the next couple of weeks my grandfather took a turn for the worst and lost his battle to lung cancer. It was horrible, more loss. I kept thinking why do all the good people in my life have to die? I was heart broken that he was gone. He had a beautiful heart and soul. He was one of the kindest men I have ever met. My grandfather always treated me like I was special, and gave me his full attention when we were together. I missed him even before he was gone.

The day of his funeral turned out to be a nightmare. We were at the cemetery, and the priest was saying his last prayers, when all of a sudden I hear this voice. A voice that totally made me shake from the inside out. In my head I was like, "OH NO," It was my mother. She came walking up, and dropped to her knees praying out loud for my grandfather's soul. "God please help him. Bring him to my son in heaven!"

My father turns to me and says, "Tell her to get the hell out of here!" I do as he says. I run up to my mother and say, "Mom get up off your knees. You have to go."

"What are you doing here?" She started screaming. She was screaming at my dad for being a bastard. Then she was screaming at an old boyfriend of hers and his wife. "I should have stayed with you, Joe. What do you think of that, bitch?" she said to his wife. "He loves me not you." Joe tried to calmly talk to her and help her to her feet, but she just spewed more foul language and spit at him.

Then I starting yelling! "Mom, get the hell out of here now, you are not welcome. Go! Just Go!" Then I started walking to the truck where my other grandfather was sitting. Of course he was drunk. I started yelling at him. Why the hell did you bring her here, she does not belong here at all. Take her home! He yelled for her to come. It was a big fiasco. In the middle of all of this my dad did not step up, or come over. He just walked away, and left me to deal with it. Same old story, looking at the back of his head! I am mortified.

I turned my attention back to my mother and forced her to get back to the truck by continually screaming at her, so she finally came over to me. I say, "Go home where you belong, Mom." She said, "Go fuck yourself go be with him and his whore!" I looked at my grandfather, "Please just take her home." He said Ok, and off they went, with her screaming obscenities out the window until they were out of sight. I walked back over to the limousine and get in. My dad was ranting about my mother. It was all a blur at this point. I just sank in the seat, and looked out the window as we drove away. I was silently saying good-bye to my grandfather, and wishing he was still here.

Two weeks after he passed away, I became deathly ill. I passed out on the kitchen floor one morning and my dad took me to the doctor. That is the day we found out I was pregnant. Those words, those horrible, horrible words ringing in my ears. Once again, he was screaming, I was crying, but I never told him one word of what really had happened to me. I felt he should have known, and he did not. I was famously silent. All the words screaming so loudly in my head just would not come out. My worst fear had just come true, I was pregnant with his demon child. His curse was still hovering over me. The words he had chanted at me over and over again were happening. I was pregnant!

Of course my dad handled it all wrong. He told my mother, who thought it was wonderful and wanted me to keep it! She wanted to raise the evil spawn growing inside me. I was about to be 14 years old, and the last thing I wanted is a baby, especially his baby, the one he wanted me to have all along. I felt God was punishing me for my life. I felt I was deemed evil too with this creature inside of me. I flipped out; I started screaming at my mother. "I hate you I hate you, I don't want this baby, I don't want you, I don't want any one of you, I hate you all!!!" I was inconsolable. My dad kicked out my mother, and left me with my grandmother (his mother) until morning. That night he tried to track down Jerry, and put the word out on the street that he was going to kill him for getting me pregnant. This was his second mistake. Now Jerry knew, and so the rumors were swirling all over town, and of course school. The one place I almost felt normal. The one place that will never be normal again once everyone hears.

Then next day he took me to the hospital, and I had an abortion. My dad was with me, he held my hand and I cried. When I woke up, it was over and all I could do was sob and say I was sorry, so sorry. Imagine, me apologizing for what they did to me. I felt it was the right thing to do. Apologize for my actions, and maybe in God's eyes I would be forgiven, and hopefully live a normal life someday. My dad was stone cold, and just glared at me. He said let's go home, and that was it. Our drive back was silent. I pretended to sleep on the way, so he wouldn't yell at me any more. I could not handle being made to feel even worse than I already did.

I thought I was going to his house but my dad took me back to my grandmother's, and dumped me off there for two days. He couldn't stand the sight of me, I could see it in his eyes. The look of disappointment burned though my soul. She took care of me. I slept like I had not slept in years, with my grandmother watching over me. I felt safe. Two days later it was my 14th birthday. I woke up on the couch with my favorite white cake sitting there. My grandmother would bake it for me every year. I smiled. She wished me a happy birthday and never said a word to me about what happened and the pregnancy. More silence. She just took care of me, and spent time with me. I wanted to talk to her about it, but I did not have the courage to bring it up to her. I so desperately wanted her to say something, anything, but she did not. She did what any good grandmother would do—she nurtured me back to health.

Then my dad came back and picked me up only to drop me back off with my mom. He didn't want me. He said I could not live with him anymore. He was having trouble with Karen and they needed to work it out, so he picked Karen over me. He said me being there was too much of a stress on their relationship, and I caused too much trouble for them. He couldn't deal with it anymore! He proved to me once again that I did not matter. He again broke my heart.

So on that day, I went to live with my mom at my grandparent's house. My mom was still unstable but getting by. This house is filled with another set of dysfunctions. My grandmother is blind, and my grandfather is a horrible drunk. My uncle is a drug addict, with his drug addict girlfriend who always crashes there, and of course, my mother.

To make matters even worse, I was forced to share a room with her sleeping in the same bed! Can you imagine having to sleep with your own mother as a teenager? They all smoked cigarettes, which I detested, so the house was always filled with smoke. It made me sick. I hated it there! So then I was thinking here we go again, out of the frying pan and into the fire.

☙ LITTLE GIRL LOST ❧

Little girl lost and alone, no where to turn, no happy
Home, only others do I see doing all this trickery...

I learn to change; I learn to hide, than nobody can see
The pain inside. Hiding behind so many masks, where
Is the real me, that is the question to ask?

Afraid of the guilt, hurt and ashamed...how did I get
Mixed up in this crazy game. Ohh these clever masks how
they hide all that is really buried so deep inside..

Shall I bring them forward for all to see, or do I keep them
For myself and fall prey to my deepest memories..

I need to shed these masks for the weight is bringing me
down, shoulders heavy, eyes tired no where to lay my
head down... How do I get away from all of my shame,
who is really to blame?

FORGIVENESS is the key, where is the door to set me free..
I need to forgive myself to get me out of this hell,
so the masks of pain can fall and break,
and I can soar through all my heartache.

Who is the real me, that is the question to ask? It's been so long I
don't truly know, it has all been one big show. So the question is
what is really left of me?

I need to fight, I need to change, I need to understand my
Pain, then I can see beyond the fantasy, OHH look over
There is that the real me?

This little girl lost needs to be found, and picked up
From the ground… The ground is not where I belong.
I deserve to be safe and warm…
I need to raise my head up high and stand tall, so all could see the real me – who is filled with wonder, who is finally FREE…

CHAPTER 9
Seeping

Chapter 9

Seeping

Here I am back at my grandmother's house. Let me give you a description of the household. This 3-bedroom ranch is up on the hill, with its long driveway, with a lot of property. Back in the day it used to be a farm and a grape vineyard. My grandfather's family owned it, and I had aunts that still lived in a little shack on the far side of the property. It was heavily grown over, but there was tons of black berry and raspberry bushes. I would go up into the woods with my cousins and pick berries all the time. There was another little house on the other side of the property, which was always rented out. The people that came through were always interesting and strange. This property on the hill was filled with much entertainment.

My family unit now consisted of my grandparents, my mother, my uncle, and his drug-infested girlfriend who would come and go. Our home was always filled with people, and not the cleanest place to be. Everyone smoked all the time, and I was the only one who did not. Family members were always visiting, and the food was endless. You know how big Italian families are, there is always a party even when there wasn't a party! There would be cookouts all hours of the night, and a lot of card playing. The house was barely ever quiet. You would think that this is ok, survivable right? Well, maybe it would have been, if I didn't have to share a room with my mother in a double bed. I had to sleep with her, and it was horrible!

She would lie on the bed and smoke all the time crying and listening to her radio. I had no privacy, no peace. Everything I owned smelled of smoke. My mother would also cough and wet herself in bed all the time. I woke up drenched in piss on several occasions. I would shower in the middle of the night, and have to change the bed. My mother would lie in her piss all night if I didn't yell and force her to get up. We were always yelling and arguing about it. I was definitely disturbed by being peed on, and I know it really screwed with my already twisted brain.

Here is the scene..

I am sound a sleep and all of a sudden I feel this warm sensation all over me. I lay there for a moment when it hits me! Not again, I say to my mother. Lisa, get over it I can't help it. Yes, you can Mom, stop smoking, wear a diaper, do something, but NO you choose to lie in your own piss and expect me to accept that. I won't, I tell you I just won't! My mother responds with, I don't care if I piss on myself, and if you don't like it go sleep somewhere else. Where the hell do you want me to go Mom, out in the fucking doghouse with Prissy? Sure go ahead you love that dog more than you love your own mother. You're right, Mom, I hate you! Do you hear me I hate you so much you wreck everything in my life I wish you were dead. My mom starts crying, and then going into a full sob, talking to God saying why me, why do I have to be punished all the time, saying this over and over again rocking back and forth. I quietly gather my things, take a shower and sit up the rest of the night with my grandfather, whose only response when I come down the hall is, did it happen again?

There was nowhere else to sleep as my grandfather was up all night in the living room, and the other bedrooms were occupied. Usually, I would end up sitting with my grandfather falling asleep on the chair, but sometimes I would climb in bed with my grandmother when I just couldn't take it anymore. I just wanted my own space. I was sick and tired of sleeping with anyone, let alone my mother. I would pray at night. God please give me my own space, help me, please help me.

Back to School

I am 14 now, and in the ninth grade. Having to return to school after the abortion was so hard for me. I lied and told people that I had mono and that is why I was out of school for 3 weeks. The stories of my pregnancy swirled all over the school. People were pointing and whispering. I stood my ground, and lied. I hated lying but I was not going to give Jerry the satisfaction of his truth! Getting me pregnant. I was adamant and held to my story. This story followed me all the way through high school. Just when I thought it was gone from my world someone would bring it up again, I could not get beyond it until after I graduated. I was branded like in the story "The Scarlet Letter," being reminded of my horrible secret over and over again, being punished for a crime that I did not commit! Was I guilty for being abused? Should I continually be punished for having my virginity ripped from me, taking away my youth? This is how I felt all the time, but I stayed tough and pushed through it all because I hoped someday it would all be just a horrible memory tucked away forever.

The strange thing is that as one goes through life after such a horrible experience, it never goes away. It is a part of you forever, and one has to learn to own it, put it in its place, and make good out of a bad situation. That lesson would be learned later on in life, with much time and work! Writing this book is part of owning who I am, and being proud of surviving all this tragedy. A wise man recently told me that I was a thriver. I looked at him funny for a moment, but I agree, what a wonderful word to use. It puts a new meaning to things on a whole new level.

What a transition period this was for me in my life.

TRANSITION

Transition that is a big word! I had so many things going on in my head, and in my broken closed off heart. I was struggling every day just to get by. I am haunted by the memories of abuse, and scared I am going to turn a corner and see Jerry standing there. I am angry at the world for wronging me, and most of all I am angry with my family for betraying me. I live in a household filled with people I feel I hate. I know in my heart I did not hate them, but at the time this is how I felt. I would argue with any one of them at a moments notice. Everything set me off. I was volatile. I was silent then explosive, and nobody could get through to me. I didn't want them to get through to me. At this point I felt, why should I talk now? Nobody cared what I had to say before, when I was in the house of horrors! I felt this was my punishment to them. This nasty side of me that I would unleash onto them everyday, payback for all that was not done to save me.

Then I would go visit my dad, and feel the same. I would step foot into my grandmother's home (his mother), and feel hatred. I tried really hard not to feel that way, but it would just come out. I would anger my dad constantly and loved it. I enjoyed watching him twitch, and make his faces before he would explode. I could guarantee it! I waited for it, and felt satisfaction watching him scream, or chase me. Sometimes I would infuriate him so bad that he would try to beat me up. I was fast, and would out run him, and that would make him even angrier.

THE PARTYING BEGINS...

I was now really starting to party. I was skipping school with my friends smoking pot, and drinking. I am tormenting other girls in school and being a bully. I was in the office and detention after school more than I was in the classroom.

In the middle of all that anger and hatred was a young girl trying to figure it all out.

I wanted to do good things, and make it on my own. I would think about my future, and what would make it better. Then the anger would come back out, and my good intentions would be put on the back burner. I was running with a group of kids somewhat like myself. They had problems at home, but not as big as mine; and I was not sharing the deep stuff. They knew about my mom and my dad, losing my brother, and that was enough. It was actually overload for other teens my age, and most didn't get it. So I would hide my pain in drugs and alcohol. Nobody knew the real me! I didn't know the real me anymore, but I was struggling to figure it out. Way down deep inside, I knew I wanted better for myself. I wanted to survive this mess, and prove to everyone I was not a loser, or scum. I was worth saving. Nobody wanted to save me, so I wanted to save myself. I wanted to laugh in all of their faces and say see I am somebody. I am worth it after all! This was my secret, my inner goal for myself. Some day it will be good for me, and I will shine like a star in the sky.

I decided it was time for me to get a job. Money is good, and it will help keep me out of my house. I found a program that works with young teens, and my first job was mopping floors at the high school pool and locker rooms twice a week. I started babysitting as well. Then I worked up at the recreation center cleaning there. During that time, I met a wonderful woman named Judy who saw something in me, and was trying to mentor me. She always came around when I was cleaning and talked to me. She asked me all sorts of questions about my life, and what my thoughts were for my future. I liked her a lot, and slowly learned to trust her. I enjoyed the attention that she always found time to give to me, just me!

I finished out the rest of my ninth grade year in school and summer was fast approaching. I actually passed ninth grade by the skin of my teeth, which totally shocked me, and everyone else. My thoughts were now turning to summer, and what I would be doing. I could not wait to get wild and crazy with my friends, and have my freedom from school.

Because I detested being home so much, I made sure that I always had something to do. So, of course, I was still partying and staying out of the house as much as possible. I was a wild child always on the go. I would walk everywhere; miles upon miles just so I didn't have to be home. I would walk 8 miles to the beach hang out and walk home at night; sometimes I would do this twice in one day.

We actually put ourselves in danger at times because we would walk home late at night and that is when all the crazies would come out. We were lucky, an angel (my brother) must have been watching over us because we were approached many times, men exposing themselves to us wanting us to get into a car or van. We were even chased on foot by this man that stalked us. It was truly a crazy time in my life—totally out of control, but I felt I was in control of my life for the first time, and I was loving it! The wilder the better, I was like bring it on, I can do anything I want, I am untouchable. Sometimes I was so outrageous and bizarre, that others would just look at me and shake their heads. Nobody really knew what to make of me, but they thought I was funny. I enjoyed that attention, being the jokester, and getting attention from everyone. It was like in the song "Free Bird" that is how I felt in those moments, and that was my signature song for sure.

A glimmer of hope…

One of the best things happened to me, Judy offered me a job at a summer camp for special needs children. She saw the spark in me to help others. She saw something in me that I didn't realize at the time. This wonderful woman extended herself to me, and wanted me to succeed. I have never had anyone in my life up until this point look at me in this light, and it affected me greatly. I wanted to do well, and be helpful. I wanted to make her proud of me. I happily agreed to work for her, and I jumped in blindly, and got the job done. I learned a lot that summer at camp, and everyone there was so kind, and willing to teach me the ropes. I was the youngest counselor there so everyone felt the need to take me under their wing. Most of the councilors were college students, so I was like the little sister everyone needed to nurture and protect. For the first time in a very long time I felt wanted and needed in a positive way, and I liked it. I was part of a team. This encouraged me to absorb everything that was put in front of me. I was like a sponge I could not get enough. I continually asked questions, and was a quick learner. I truly enjoyed all of the children, and being a part of this special group of people. I worked Monday thru Friday all summer, this the summer before I started high school.

I would work all day, come home eat shower and then go out all night. My mother was always trying to track me down, and I was on the move. I was hanging out with my friends, and partying like a rock star! Jerry was tucked away in the back of my mind, and as long as I was on the move, I didn't have to think about him. Feeling this new sense of freedom gave me fuel to keep on pushing forward. I did not want to listen to anyone, and I was defiant as ever on the home front. A place that made me feel completely miserable, and forced me to think about my past. So I ran all the time. Running was my best defense from my thoughts, and my home situation. My mother was still crazy as ever. She would constantly yell at me, and she would chase me down all the time. When she would find me she would beat me up right in front of my friends. I didn't care, I felt freedom and it was worth it.

This is the scene…

Here I am walking down Ocean Avenue one night with my best friend Allie, and my mother pulls up and gets out of her car. I look at Allie and say, "Oh, shit." My mother marches up to me screaming, have you been drinking, Lisa? I say, no Mom, I have not. Yes you have, you liar, and smacks me right across my face. Allie stood in fear, as she has witnessed this countless times before. Mom, I start screaming ,leave me alone go home, just go home. No Lisa, get in the car we are going home now do you hear me! You are an alcoholic just like your grandfather and worthless. She turns to Allie and screams get in the car, I will take you home, your mother doesn't want you out wandering the streets like a call girl. Allie gets in with me, as we didn't want a further scene to be caused. Once in the car my mother is now ranting and raving about sin, alcoholics and whores! We just endure it sitting in the back seat like two little kids being scolded. We are silent, and just looking at each other, reading our eyes as my mother drove 90 miles and hour to Allie's house. As soon as my mom pulls up to the house she jumps out quick, mouthing to me, "I'm sorry." This was so typical, and happened so many times. It was bizarre!

This did not stop me it only made it worse. I would come home after a night of partying, and my mother and I would get into it really bad. When I think back now, my poor grandmother being blind, and having to hear my mother and I battling, I feel bad. We would bang off the walls going down the hallway. My grandmother would be yelling at both of us to stop! My mother would continually whack me the whole way down that hall, and I would block her. Some nights that hall seemed extra long, and as I was being smashed I would think to myself will this ever end. Believe it or not I never once hit her back. I knew it was not the right thing to do even though I wanted to so badly. I wanted to just smash the shit out of her, but I just blocked her and took my beatings. I wanted her to feel the pain like I felt for so long, but I just couldn't bring myself to hit her. Deep down inside I knew she was sick and could not help herself. I still had respect for her, being my mother, even though at this moment in my life I hated her.

I would also fight terribly with my grandfather, because he would come home drunk, and be so obnoxious; I just couldn't take it. I had a short fuse, especially when it came to him. The way he would treat my grandmother, it was so demeaning. After all the abuse I took from Jerry, I couldn't stand to see anyone else is that same situation. This was my grandmother, and no matter how much of a hard time I gave her, I loved her dearly, she was a tough woman. She deserved better.

My grandmother would always say to me Lisa, promise me you will not fight with him today as it will not get you anywhere. I promise Grandma, I won't. I will just be quiet. I really did try! Then he would come in the door and start picking on all of us. Then he would be so mean to my grandmother, and I would lose it. I could not stand the way he was treating her. She did not deserve it, and I felt like I needed to protect her. I remember thinking to myself, "I need to do something to take the attention off of her."

I would start by mouthing off to him, and we would start fighting viciously like pit bulls at each other's throats. The battles would get quite heated, and at this point, everyone would be yelling the dysfunction was astounding. One time he was so angry with me, that he threw his false teeth at me. They broke all over the floor, teeth were flying everywhere. I was laughing at him telling him, taunting him with sarcasm, and saying, "Good, that is what you get old man." At the same time my grandmother was crying, and my mom was screaming and ranting, waving her fists at the sky cursing God for all that was happening. Sounds like a lovely scene, doesn't it? It always ended with me running out of the house, and meeting up with my friends and getting hammered. On the occasions that is was extremely late, I would steal my mom's car, pick up my best friend and go joy riding all night long. Every day was a mess, and I just kept on running, and time just kept on moving..

THE WEDDING DAY

My dad finally got married to Karen. My mom put a lot of pressure on me not to go to that wedding. She would say all sorts of horrible things to me, like I will rot in Hell if I go, or I will curse you forever! She was scary with her wicked tongue and crazy eyes telling me how my brother was crying in heaven because of my father's betrayal. She would wave her fist at me and tell me that I better not ever betray her or I would be beaten senseless. I would hear this everyday. She even went on to say, she would scratch my eyes out if she needed to. So demented, and disturbing.

Our conversation would go like this…

I am sitting at the kitchen table eating my breakfast, and my mother walks in and sits down with her coffee lights a cigarette and glares at me. I ignore her hoping she will not start on me, as always I am wrong about something.

"So, are you going to the wedding?' my mother asks, and goes on to say, " You know if you go, you will rot in hell, you little bitch!" I look at her and say, "No Mom, I'm not going" and my tone is short and to the point. "I do not believe you, Lisa, you lie all the time, and God will punish you if you lie to me. He will cut out your tongue." "Mom, I am not going so please stop now it's ok." Then here comes the explosion…

"Liar, liar, liar,' my mom is screaming, fists banging on the table, coffee spilling everywhere. I get up and start screaming at her, "STOP it you stupid bitch ,I am not going and that is the end of it, now leave me the fuck alone!"

My grandmother enters the room, hearing the commotion, and she starts yelling at my mother. "Joann, leave Lisa alone, let her get ready for school now end it!" My mother looks at me with her evil eyes and says, "We will talk later, I love you now get ready for school, sweetheart." I walk away.

This is a description of countless moments from my childhood, and what I had to live with every day.

Then she would say other things like, I hope your father dies, and would call his bride to be all sorts of choice words! Yes, this Catholic woman, a child of God speaking with such trashy dialogue. One of her many personalities coming out when she was mad, switching it up every time the words flowed from her lips. Not only would the words switch up but her facial expressions as well. You could watch her transform into her different personas. It was scary and animated at the same time. It sounds almost unbelievable, but it is true. You would have to be in the moment to witness it, to get the full-blown reality of Joann, and this illness that has wrecked her brain. It was like watching a 3-d movie. Imagine Godzilla or King Kong larger than life in your face, as you are frozen in fear, but shocked at the same time at what you are actually witnessing. I think that is the best way that I could describe the moment.

LATER THAT DAY...

I come home from school, and she is sitting at the table waiting for me. I walk in the door and dread comes over my face. I take one look at her and she is ready to pick up from where we left off this morning...

"You have a good day at school sweetheart," my mom says? I say "Yes mom it was fine, and I need to do my homework before I go to work." " Ok Lisa you do that, and think about all the tears flowing from heaven because your brother is crying. He is sad and angry with your rotten father." "Mom, Dad is not rotten and Jon Jon is not crying he is at peace!' " Don't you tell me what your brother is, you little fuck! He is crying because your father left us and now he is marrying that whore bag!" " Mom, stop please I know you're upset about the wedding I promise I will not go, ok?" "Ok, Lisa because you know what will happen if you do?" " I know, Mom, I will rot in hell, right?" " Yes, that is correct so go get your homework done, and then you can go to work." She says this in a snide voice, and she goes on to say "Are you hungry I can make you a snack?" " No thanks, I'm good just let me do what I need to do!"

As I walk away my mother calls to me, and when I turn around she gives me the finger and starts singing this song she made up about a monkey's asshole. I shake my head in disgust and go to my room.

The wedding night...

As they were getting married, I was getting drunk in the bathroom of the roller-skating rink—cherry brandy! I was in the stall crying and drinking. As always I was alone, this was my famous trademark. Again, the only time I would let out my emotions was when I was drunk and alone. I felt weak when I cried, and I hated that feeling. I was so conflicted that I did not want to be involved in any part of their wedding, and I was extremely angry. The thought of them being married made me sick to my stomach. I resented Karen for taking my dad away from me. I hated my dad for once again putting me on the back burner feeling he was selfish and one sided for not putting me first in his life. My refusal to go to the wedding made him quite disappointed, and that was my wedding present to him, sadness. I wanted him to feel the hurt and sadness that I have endured for so long. I wondered if I was even a second thought to him on that day. Was my absence even noticed? Did he even care? He did not insist that I be there, it wasn't an issue. He was mad but left it alone. My dad was so ready to move on, that if I didn't want to keep up the pace of following him, I would be left in the dust.

It was not long before they were having their trials as a married couple. It was all about drinking and going to the bar for them. Summer softball leagues, my dad bartending and bouncing at different bars. I would go visit him when he was working, and he would give me alcohol. That was our connection. Me sitting at the end of the bar talking to adults drinking feeling all grown up, until one night when an older man hit on me, my dad threw him through the screen door of the bar. My father flipped out, but what did he expect when you bring a teen into a bar situation and feed them alcohol?

Another friend of my father kissed me, and wanted to take me out. The bar is definitely not a place to raise a child, and I was living the lifestyle first hand. I would still argue with him, but not as much. I just accepted the fact that he chose his new wife and new lifestyle over me, and I tried to find a way to fit into that. I felt on some levels I fit in when I was at the bar. It was a common ground for us, and after a drink or two I didn't care. I loved my dad very, very much, and no matter how much he devastated me, I wanted that relationship in my life. I gave up a lot to get that relationship. I took all my pain and anger, rage, and disappointment and locked it away so I could just love this man. Don't get me wrong, there were a lot of times that I would act out and be angry throughout this process, but the bottom line was, I wanted my dad. To me it was worth it to have him in my life. I needed to have one real parent in my world. I desperately needed it. Our relationship was part of my survival.

I also believe I was able to put it all aside because I had always wanted him to be the one to save me. I guess everyone's childhood fantasy! I wanted my dad to be my hero! I rationalized my thoughts, as him being in my life was a positive not a negative. I never wanted to let go of my love for him, and I never did! Something inside me told me never let go. Was it my brother? Was it my deep sense of family? Or was it a young girl who just needed her father? I feel it is all of the above.

Somehow through all of the pain, I felt his real love for me, and I understood his pain. As young as I was, I always understood his pain. My thoughts were always brought back to the moment, when my brother died, and I was stroking my father's hair as he sobbed in my lap. I was six years old with a deep understanding of life. On some crazy levels I still idolized him. Big John, everyone was afraid of him, as he was a crazy man. He was never afraid of anything or anyone. He was an icon in our town. He was larger than life! His only fears were at night in his sleep where he was silently tortured by all his shortcomings and past pains. Those dreams stayed with him until he passed away. I know his dreams were because of his silent pain, his silent torture that he never spoke of. It was there and I knew it, I felt it, and he knew I was aware of it always. We did have a special connection that nobody else ever had, and I believe it was because of our similar silence, that only came alive in our dreams…

Time went on…

I worked hard and I played hard, and before I knew it summer was over, and off to high school I went. I had my two best friends by my side, and we moved forward together. Young, wild, and free! That is how we all felt back then. As they say, "Youth holds no bounds!" I was still working for Judy, and loving it. I cleaned at the recreation center, and then the bowling league for the handicapped. This was something I felt good about. Judy always had a way of talking to me that made me feel good about myself. She was and incredible mentor. When I was at work I was at my best, but school was another story.

I was immediately struggling in high school because of the partying. We drank and smoked pot before school, during school, and after school. Then we started experimenting with pills. Uppers, downers, pain killers—we tried it all. When I think back, it amazes me how easy it was to get them. We also got a lot bolder. Some of our antics were off the chart. One time we tied a kid to a tree and forced his cousin to go buy us alcohol. I used to bully this young man and take his skate board and radio from him, and made him pay me to get his items back. This was another way I could make money to support my habit. It was also another way that I felt in control. I am not proud of it looking back now, but at that time frame I just didn't care. We stole things from the store all the time, and even took diet pills to get high. One day my friends and I split a whole box, and stayed up for two days straight. I thought my heart was going to bang out of my chest. I was speeding so badly, and totally paranoid. It was an awful experience. There was nothing we would not try. We even snorted speed a few times. I thought my head was going to pop off. I hated the feeling, and I learned quickly that snorting things up your nose was a big no no! I never did it again, as it was just too much for me to handle.

On another occasion we found an open door to a vacant store, and we went in to explore. In the back room there was a hole in the wall to a clothing store. We couldn't believe our eyes! We saw dollar signs, thinking this is our jackpot. We crawled on our stomachs, and started taking all the clothing. One of our friends went and got a shopping cart in the plaza and we loaded it up. Imagine the scene. There are 5 of us, high and laughing so loud, I am surprised nobody heard us. We are crawling on the floor on our hand and knees pulling stuff off the racks and stuffing them through the hole. We were like kids in a candy story grabbing everything we can. It is dark, and the adrenaline was pumping. I could remember feeling my heart pounding so hard in my chest, my mind racing, ears ringing. What a rush, a combination of fear and excitement. The thought of new clothing, and money! We managed to take a lot of stuff, and get away without being seen or heard. We ran with the shopping cart filled with stuff to my friend's house. We came in the door, and her parents were just as excited when we told them what we did. They were not good people, and took control of the situation. They told us take some of the things that we wanted, and the rest they would sell and keep the money. We were pissed, and I did mouth off to the parents but they kicked me out. With my clothing in hand, I was shoved out the door. I banged on the door and called them some choice words, but they didn't even respond, so I just left. They did go on to sell all of the stuff we stole, and made great money. I guess this was our punishment for doing something so wrong. A learning lesson for sure! This experience was another thing I could be pissed about, and feel that the world had did me wrong again. My rage burned! I would say things to my friend all the time, but she would just say that's my parents I am sorry, and finally I just let it go. I moved forward onto more trouble.

The next step was stealing my grandfather's painkillers. We would take 5 or 6 at a time, plus drink!

Let me share this conversation with you…

I am sitting at my kitchen table, the famous spot where all the action usually happened. My grandmother was sitting there as always knitting. Yes, this blind woman knitted as well. She did everything. She would say to me all the time, "You know, Lisa, if I could see I would drive right out of here, and never come back!" I would say, "Can I come with you?" She would always say, "Yes of course."

Then in walks my grandfather, he has just woken up from a nap. He is rummaging through the cabinet, getting frustrated.

"Hey Rose, where are all my painkillers? Jesus Christ where the hell did they go?"

My grandmothers response, 'Pat you probably took them all and do not remember!"

"Bull shit I would remember taking them," and he is now getting irate. "Oh Pat, you probably took them when you were drunk, as you are quite often and forgot, it doesn't surprise me at all, just order more." " When am I drunk, he spouts?" " Everyday, Pat, Every day." He storms off, and my grandmother turns to me and says, "The truth hurts doesn't it!" " Yes, Grandma it does and I smile." I smile for two reasons, for one she is totally right as she usually was, and I just got away with taking all the pills. I do have to say sitting there during this conversation, I was nervous waiting for the hammer to drop on my head so to speak.

Party, Party, Party…

I remember sitting on the beach by myself looking up at the sky crying, spaced out of my mind on pills and booze. This was the only time I would actually let out anything that I was feeling. I would talk to my brother sitting on that beach our private meeting spot. I felt he always knew when I would be there, and he was waiting for me. Like in the movie "Charlie St. Cloud." It was about a young man who would go into the woods and play ball, and talk with his deceased brother. When I saw the movie myself I totally related to it, as I did the same thing. I was always alone when I did this, as I never wanted to show weakness to others. Then there were other times when I would just get crazy, and brake bottles cutting myself. I beat up a dumpster one evening and fractured my hand. I would get these bursts of anger through the haze of partying and flip out for no apparent reason. Nobody understood it, but they just went with it. I punched my hand through a glass window in an abandoned house where we were partying one night. I was always good for the extreme totally impulsive and unexpected.

One evening we were walking and passed a car with the window down, and the keys in the ignition. At this stage of my life I was a professional driver! I said let's steal the car and go for a joy ride. We were all high, as we just smoked a bunch of weed. My friends agree, and we jump in. I was behind the wheel feeling free as a bird, blasting the radio and off we went. We went all over town, laughing and joking the whole way. When we were done, I told them we had to put the car back. They thought I was crazy, but I had this deep sense of righteousness inside me, and was thinking who ever owns this car obviously needs it back. I drove the car back to where it was parked, my friends were screaming at me the whole way afraid we were going to get caught, but I didn't care, all I could think about was the person who owned it having to go to work in the morning. This is mind blowing! I am 14, baked out of my mind, and I am thinking of the owner of the vehicle and the right thing to do. This is how I was, always thinking, and wanting to make sure things were ok. Even at my worst, I was always trying to do my best.

Sophomore year seemed to be flying by. I was making it through by the skin of my teeth, as my grades were horrible. I was barely passing, and I just didn't care. All I wanted to do was party, and hang out with my friends, and that is what I focused on. I had a few boyfriends here and there, but I really didn't want one. I was so damaged by Jerry, that I felt I could not trust any of them. I would go on a date or a boy would kiss me, and all the images would come flooding back to me. I couldn't handle it. The flashbacks were brutal. Guys thought I was either a prude, or a tease. I felt bad. This was not the case at all, but I could not express myself, or explain why I was the way I was. I would think maybe I could have a normal relationship with a boy, but once it started I would flip because of the flashbacks. They were so disgusting. It was like a picture show in my mind, so vivid and real. Sometimes I was actually reliving the moments of abuse, and could not get out of it. I always ended my relationships quick because of it. I learned to block it out totally, and pretended that part of my life never happened. I would continually train myself to forget it all, and that is what I did. I focused more on my friends, and staying out of my house as much as possible.

Winter was now upon us, and it made it harder to get out because I would walk everywhere. It was freezing at the beach, but we would endure it often. We made friends with older kids who drove, and we would go riding all night. We moved the party indoors, so to speak. Piled in a car, partying, driving crazy, loud music, and just mayhem. I was used to mayhem, so this didn't bother me at all, except when the driver used to fall asleep because he was so baked! We had a few near misses, but one night when I was lucky enough not to be in the car he fell asleep and crashed it. Unfortunately, my cousin was in the car, and a terrible tragedy occurred—the death of a young man. This image would stay with my cousin forever. We were all young and foolish, truly we thought we were invincible. What an awful lesson to have to learn. Many of us learned the hard way.

Even through the craziness I was still working and loving what I was doing. I visited my dad once or twice a week, and tolerated his lifestyle with his wife. I also saw my other grandmother and aunt. When I was stuck home, I was miserable.

I would be stuck in a house so filled with smoke you could cut it with a knife, and I was sick quite often. I just kept on enduring it. I think the worst part of it all was to continually share a room with my mother. She was relentless! Up all hours of the night smoking, crying, and praying. Imagine sharing a bed with your parent at 15 years old. This situation went on for the next few years, and really messed with my head.

I was so embarrassed by it, and did not share this information with anyone. Some nights I would wake up and she would be praying over me for my safety. I would hear her chanting prayers in my ear; she would almost sound demonic the way she did it. I would tell her to shut the hell up, and then she would swear at me, her mouth was nasty and foul for such a good Christian woman. I felt this was the inner demon called mental illness, so deep inside of her coming out. She was always on the edge, and you would never know when it would surface. I was getting really good at figuring her out. I knew all of her moods, and personalities. I would taunt her at times, as I knew what she would do next. She did a lot of repetitive things so she was predicable at times. Other times it was a crapshoot, and I should have just kept my mouth shut, as I would expect one thing and get something totally different. I did learn how to talk to her on many different levels, but in the end when it turned bad, I would catch a beating. On a few occasions she actually chased me with big scissors threatening to stab me. She seemed to fancy those scissors, so I got smart and threw them away.

Change of Seasons

I survived the winter, and the nicer weather was here, so I was back on the move, walking everywhere again. I make it through the school year and actually passed again. My grades were slightly better this time around.

I am still working for Judy, and getting ready to start the summer program at the camp again. I feel I am at my best when I am with the kids. My ability for compassion was incredible considering all I have been through. One would think that I would be so hardened and unfeeling, but I was the opposite. I wanted to make a difference with these children; I felt it in my bones. A young girl wanting to make it better for others, and give them what she didn't have—compassion!

As summer begins, big news hits. I find out that my stepmother is pregnant. It is a bittersweet moment for me. On one level I am upset, thinking another reason for my dad not to be with me, and happy because I will have a sibling. I lost my brother so many years ago, and was robbed of that time with him. I do not want to tell my mother, because she will flip out. I keep it to myself for a little bit.

Off to work I go, first day of camp. I meet a new little girl named Debbie, and her younger sister. Debbie was about 8 yrs old with long blond hair, blue eyes, and a big crooked smile. She was a little slow, as her mother was an alcoholic and drank through the whole pregnancy. She is standing there before me unaware of her ragged clothing and dirty hair. She is oblivious to it all, as she is smiling and taking in all the activity around her. My heart went out to this child immediately. I took her under my wing, and she loved me. We became fast friends, and I would look forward to seeing her every day. I worked one on one with her, helping her with her math and reading skills. We ran and played and

I taught her how to throw a ball and worked on her coordination. My camp leader was quite impressed with the work I was doing with her and encouraged it.

I remember getting paid, going to the store, and buying Debbie some new clothing. It was ninety degrees out, and she would come to camp with winter clothing on. They constantly talked to her mother about it, but it continued. I took it upon myself to buy her summer clothing. I also brought shampoo and soap to the camp, and when we would go to the pool I would shower her and wash her hair. I bought her a brush and would untangle her long knotted hair. She was so happy to be clean. She gave me big hugs and smiled brightly. I actually met her mother, and asked if Debbie could come to my house and hang out with me, and she agreed. Typical drunk! She did not care where her kids were as long as they were out of her hair. I took her all the time. I would bathe her at my home, and buy her new clothing and art supplies. Debbie loved to draw and paint, and so did I, we had a blast together. I was even invited to her birthday party, and gave her new shoes, socks, underwear, and toys. I even bought her brother and sister gifts as well. The mother seemed grateful and quite drunk. I would stop buy her house from time to time, when I was walking and she always welcomed me in. I felt the need to check up on this child, as nobody else seemed to care. Her living conditions were horrible, and I did make a complaint to the camp leaders. They stated they reported it, but I really do not think they did, because nothing was changing.

Summer went by quick and things were changing. I still hung out down at the beach at night, and partied; but it was starting to get old. I engrossed myself in my work and this child. My thought process was starting to change. I was thinking of my future, and wanting to be a good role model for my new sibling on the way. My thoughts were becoming less clouded, and I was becoming more aware of people being affected by my actions. I had a boyfriend for a while, but he ended up cheating on me with my best friend. This hurt me tremendously, but it came down to sex. I was 15, and not into it. After all I had been through, I just couldn't take the relationship to that next level. Even though it ended badly the relationship was the first step for me to figure out what a real relationship should be like. We had some good moments, and I actually learned how to enjoy the company of a young man on a positive level. He was kind to me, and made me feel good about myself, which was something I had never felt before from a boy.

My so-called friend is the same one whose parents took our stuff and sold it. It was yet another learning lesson for me. She actually dated another one of my old boyfriends later on in the year, and her and I got into a physical altercation. We ended our friendship for good. My friends, my party buddies, were not really my friends, and once summer was over we all started going our separate ways. The beach crew was breaking up, and some of us were growing up, and some of us were not!

Summer camp ended, and Debbie and her family ended up moving away. I was heartbroken and worried. Staff members assured me that a report was filed against her mother. They told me social services were on the case. I was able to get updates about Debbie for about a year, and then they moved never to be heard from again.

I would often think of her, and smile. She was a pure joy, brought into my world at a time when I needed something to help me change. She was my angel who came in at the right time, and showed me what it was like to feel again. I would pray at night that she was safe.

They say people come in and out of our lives for a reason, and this proves that phrase to be the truth. I did learn a lesson, one that I will never forget.

Back to high school junior year…

SEEPING

Seeping, creeping all flooding in,
Those crazy emotions can't hold them,
Walls so Thin...

Remaining in control, when the flood
Gates open wide, how do I relieve
The hurt inside...

Wanting to share, shake my tree...
Leaves falling so bear for all to see...

Cleansing my soul with the new falling
Snow, what a long path needing to go.

Shedding the iceberg surrounding my
Heart, knowing my family is all torn apart...

Alone I stand on this dam of destruction...
Who will be my contractor start new
Construction of my heart that is torn
So deep, pain pouring out how long
Will it seep...

CHAPTER 10

Changing Seasons

Chapter 10

Changing Seasons

Fall has come once again, and it is junior year! I head back to school with a new attitude. Something inside me has definitely changed. After this past summer, I am seeing things through new eyes, and a fresh perspective. I am thinking of my future, and what steps I need to take to change things for myself and have a better life.

I want to be a better person, and I know that I can be. I am starting to put old behaviors to rest, as they have not helped me at all. I feel that I can possibly have a positive relationship with men, and I want to try. My mother is still my mother, but as long as I keep on moving and stay busy I can control my feelings. The less that I am home, and doing productive things, the better off I will be. I am getting mentally stronger every day, and figuring out what will help me. I do not ask anyone for help, I figure it all out on my own. I am determined to make it.

I put my energy into my studies, and it starts to pay off. My first semester I received honors, and I was so excited. A lot happened to me in the first semester of junior year. I was working two jobs, got my license, and had a car. The car gave me another level of freedom. I was pleased. I had a physical altercation with my so-called best friend right in the cafeteria at school. Not one fight but two. We were both suspended for 10 days. I was so angry. I did not want to be out of school for 10 days, I had work to do. So, I took it upon myself to go to school and sit with the guidance counselor and plead my case. I explain how my friend approached me, and hit me first. I did not want to fight, but felt compelled because she attacked me. The second fight she approached me again, and even sat at my lunch table taunting me. I just snapped, and before I knew it I jumped over the table, put her in a headlock, and punched her in the face repeatedly until they finally broke us up. Yes, this was wrong, but I explained that life has been hard for me, and my anger got the best of me. The counselor seemed impressed by my honesty and maturity for coming in, and reduced my suspension to 3 days. I walked out of his office feeling proud of myself for handling things the right way. He did offer for me to come speak with him about my problems, but I politely thanked him and declined. I was doing this on my own; I felt I did not need anyone else's help ever! I was a loner out there in the world making my way one step at a time. I felt that if I let people in to try to help, they might be too judgmental of me. I also felt so much shame from the sexual abuse that I did not want to say it out loud. I did not want to hear those words float off my lips. It was better for me to do it on my own. I felt more in control of my feelings that way.

I also met a great guy in math class. His name was Mark. The first time I saw him, I thought wow, he is so cute. He stared at me all the time, and everyone noticed. He was a year younger than me, but that didn't bother me. We started talking, and hit it off right away. Not only was he cute, but he was kind and compassionate as well. He came from an upper middle class family, and he had an older sister in my grade. His parents were together and hardworking. I was totally attracted to the whole package. This is the type of family I longed for my whole life. The white picket fence, *Leave it to Beaver* kind of family. It didn't take long for us to start dating, and I felt on top of the world. We became serious as a couple, and fell in love.

I am 16 yrs old, in love for the first time, and I am working my ass off. It felt fabulous. I was starting to regain some of my self-esteem. As I was making my way through junior year I lost another friend. She was my absolute best friend from kindergarten, Allie. When I had the altercation with my other friend, she decided to side with her, and dumped me. This was another loss, and I was sad. We had gone through so much together. She was by my side through all our trials and troubles on the streets. We did everything together until now. I kept on thinking, another loss, why me? Why do I lose everything I love? It hurt a lot, but I was not going to let it stop me. I kept pushing forward. I had to let go of a piece of my past. It was extremely heartbreaking.

March came in like a lion, and the day after my brother's birthday, my sister was born. Ironic, my brother's birthday was March 17th, and now my new baby sister was born on March 18th. I was ecstatic. I felt my brother was giving me a sign. With her birth being the next day, it was like he was saying, it is time to heal. I could hear him saying to me be a good role model for her, and help guide her. Love her always! That is exactly what I felt inside. So I did what my heart told me to do; I loved her with every ounce of my being. I was never jealous of her not once.

I loved spending time with her, and she wanted to spend time with me. She would get excited when I would come visit, and that made me feel so happy. I had a sibling that loved me. Even though she was just a baby I felt like she just accepted me, as I was, no explanation necessary.

I started having issue with my stepmother in regards to my sister. She was a new mother and fiercely protective of my sister. She did not trust me with her at all. She was afraid I was going to be jealous and hurt her. I was angry with her for feeling this way about me. I would never hurt my sister, why would I? I already lost one sibling. I certainly did not want to lose another. I wanted to be a good role model for her. I wanted to say these things to Karen, but instead I just internalized my anger once again. My inability to express myself was definitely a deficit in my life, as nobody ever knew what I was really thinking or feeling. I was looked at as an angry teen. Nobody thought wow she is a young woman that is so hurt and damaged by her past that she cannot even talk about it.

When I look back at things now, I do realize she was just being a protective mother. My behavior was truly awful and unpredictable for so long who could blame her. She could not see past my walls that I put up, and she only saw my angry side. We had many disagreements in regards to my sister that first year of her life, and I was limited on the time I could spend with her. That hurt me a lot, but I kept on going.

This fueled me even more to do well. I wanted to show everyone that I could make it on my own, and be a great person. I continued to work hard, and spent a lot of time with my boyfriend and his family. I loved being around them, and in my mind I pretended that they were my family. They were open and accepting, and very loving. The extended family was just as kind, and I fit right in for the first time in my life. They gave me acceptance and unconditional love. I felt safe when I was with them.

My mother of course was not happy with any of this, and reminded me every chance she got that they were not my family. I think at times she took great satisfaction in hurting me. She would put this look on her face when she would say things, and it was like hurting me empowered her.

One morning when I was getting ready for school she says to me, "You know Lisa you are never here anymore." I was like, "Sorry, I have been busy." She then looks at me with that nasty glare, and states, "If you try to leave this family I will find you and kill you!" Mom, knock it off! I am not doing this with you; do you hear me? She ignores me and says, "I mean it, and if you think that whore bag is your mother now, I will stab her too, I mean it, you ungrateful little bitch! I am the one who raised you, and I am the best mother in the whole world, and you will obey me!" I can feel myself boiling on the inside, the best mother in the world, what world, the world of the crazies? I calmly turn to her and say, "Mom, you know I love you, and you are the only mother I will ever have, so please stop so I can get ready for school." She looks at me with one eye closed, a smirk on her face, and says, "Ok, Lisa but if you are lying..." I cut her off before she can finish and say, Love you, Mom! I learned how to play the game with her. This is how I coped with living with her. Using my words carefully to play her like a fiddle, keeping her in line, and off my back. Most of the time it worked, but when she would really get under my skin, and I could not hold my composure, that is when it would get really bad.

I was constantly training myself to hold it together. I would practice it, keeping my composure at all costs. Learning how to hide my true feelings, and playing the part of the obedient daughter. This coping skill saved me countless times in the moment, but the long-term affects were damaging. In my adult life, not being able to express my true emotions caused so many problems. How was I to know what this behavior would do to my future, as I did not have anyone to tell me any different! I can confidently and firmly say now, NEVER, use this method to get through difficult situations, always express what is truly in your heart. As they say, the truth will set you free... words to live by.

My mom would also harass me about my new sister all the time. She would say all sorts of horrible things about my father and his newfound family. I would lash out at her from time to time, because she was so relentless about it. This would infuriate me because every time I would build up my wall, she would rip it down with her heinous words burning straight through to my heart. When I would explode, it always turned ugly. The vicious things we would say to each other. She would smash me over and over again with her open hand. Other times she would throw things at me, or grab me and shake me. I would run from the house, and drive off like a maniac crying. Once again, I was put in a dangerous position at the hands of my mentally ill mother.

When I would calm down I would be disappointed in myself for losing control.

I would then pull myself together, tuck it away like it never happened, and move on with my day. These incidents would happen before school, before work, or before going out with my friends. I would hide it, and nobody would ever know. This pain that sat heavy on my heart daily was my private hell. Of course I would share with my boyfriend some things, but not all. He was well aware of how my mother was and he detested her. He was comforting, and supportive as best as he could be.

I would get up every day, and put on a brave face, and tackle the world. I engrossed myself in all the positive things I could be a part of. I would run out of the house early in the morning, stop home after school, and then run out until late at night. This was my pattern for survival! I would visit my dad a couple of times a week, and my grandmother. Most of the time we would all meet at her house for dinner. My sister would always be there, and I looked forward to our time together. My boyfriend would come as well, and they all loved him. He was great with my family, both sides actually. He was very patient, and understanding for a young man. He gave me great support, and I did lean on him a lot.

Spring was now in full bloom, and off to the junior prom we went. I bought the most beautiful white gown with my own money, and I was so proud. I worked hard and it felt good to reward myself with such a beautiful dress. I felt like a princess when I put it on. We both wore all white, like the purity of our relationship. I valued every moment we spent together, and felt it was a gift from God for all that I had been through. Prom was incredible, and before we knew it junior year was over.

I did not return to the camp that summer. I decided to work at a grocery store instead to make more money, and get more hours. I felt bad about not returning, but I did promise that in the fall I would go back to the bowling program and help out. I enjoyed working at the grocery store and made some new friends along the way. Summer was going by quickly, and I did go on vacation with my boyfriend and his family to

Wildwood, NJ. That was their yearly adventure, and the extended family was there as well. We had a blast, and I was happy.

My own family was the same as usual. When I was home on the rare occasion, I would talk with my grandmother, who always had interesting things to say. She was a very smart woman, with a lot of wisdom. I know she didn't think I was listening to her, but I really was. I did admire her for her strength and courage.

She would always tell me to be strong, and fight. She would say, "Lisa, you will catch more flies with honey than vinegar!" I actually looked forward to our conversations over coffee. I let my guard down and we became extremely close.

Looking back now, I cherish those moments, and I can still hear her talking to me, and giving me advice. I remember all of her stories from her childhood, and I now realize just how sassy she was. I am a lot like her! Wow, what a realization.

Then there was my grandfather, always doing the same things. He was now retired, but still drinking every day. He was a junk man who always went trash picking. He would fix things up and sell them. He was quite good at what he did, and he was very resourceful. He was busy all the time now doing his own little things. We were not arguing as much anymore, he seemed to be more controlled with his alcohol and not hitting the bar like he used to. He did his drinking at home a lot, but only beer and wine, so he didn't get all crazy and out of control. I actually started to form a bond with him over beers late at night when I would come home, and he was the only one up. We would watch late night movies, and talk about life. He would tell me many stories about his family and his upbringing. He would tell me how they were so poor he would put cardboard in his shoes because of the holes, or how he would sleep in the barn in the hay, because it was warmer than the house. He would have to share one bedroom with all of his siblings there were 8. The girls were on one side, and boys on the other. His father was abusive, and his mother worked on the farm like a slave. His oldest brother jumped on a train car one night and didn't return for years. They were all musically inclined, and sang and played many different types of instruments. They had a grape arbor on the side of the house, and made homemade wine and moonshine. The stories were endless, and quite interesting.

He would go on and on with stories of the Mafia in Italy, and how our family came over on the boat to get away from them. Some of our ancestors were killed at the hands of the Mafia, and it sounded like something out of a storybook. The way that my grandfather would tell a story, big expressive eyes with various tones in his voice was quite captivating. He knew how to hold your attention, and could be quite charismatic when he wanted to be. He was also very funny, the way he would look at you while he was talking, you couldn't help but smile.

My uncle moved out, and we were no longer subjected to the drug-infested girlfriend. That was a bonus for our family as she truly was a train wreck. I know my grandmother was happy that she was gone, but felt bad that my uncle moved on. The house was still busy with family coming and going constantly.

My cousins would come up daily, and work with my grandfather with his junk.

They also went crabbing and fishing a lot. I went with them once in a while, but I was mainly focused on being away from home. At this point there were actually some positive things going on.

I started to spend a little bit more time with my dad and his family. I enjoyed my time with my sister, and my stepmother was noticing my behavior change. I had earned her trust, and finally she allowed me to baby sit. I was over the moon. I mean I babysat many other children, but was not allowed to babysit my own family member and that disturbed me. I was great with her, and she loved me so much. She would be so excited to see me, and that felt great. We formed a special bond that could never be broken. Things were moving along in a positive direction.

I did have a set back emotionally, when one day at work a young woman came up to me and stated that she was dating Jerry, and she knew who I was. When I heard those words it was like someone punched me in the stomach, I lost all my air. I felt like I was choking. I knew who she was, we were in high school together, but I did not know she was dating him. I thought he was in New York, but he came back. I managed to get some words out, but I was stuttering. I asked her, "Why do you feel the need to tell me about him?" She wanted to let me know that he talked about me all the time, and that he was hers now! I just laughed and said, "OK, you can have him!" She went on to say, that if I came any where near him she was going to beat me up. I am thinking this girl hunted me down at work to tell me this bullshit. I was enraged, and I told her that I wanted NO part of him ever, and if she were smart she would stay away because he was a horrible person. Well, I hit the nerve button, and she was on the verbal attack. She went on to say, that I was the horrible slut who broke his heart and had an abortion. She told me she was going to tell everyone what a whore I was when we returned to school.

I just looked at her and said, "You just don't understand," and I went off crying, running into the bathroom at work. I sat on the floor hyperventilating. Rocking and crying just like the old days. This incident put me right back to where I was when I was with my mom at my old house. I was getting instant flashbacks, and broke into a full anxiety attack. The sweat was pouring down my face, and trickled down my chest and spine. I had to get out of there, but I was afraid to move. Was Jerry with her? Was he waiting for me outside? He now knows where I work, is he going to stalk me? I totally flipped out. I managed to get myself up, and went to my boss I lied and said I had a family emergency, my mother was in the hospital, and I had to leave. He gave me the ok, and off I ran. Here I am running again. This is all I seem to do is run.

I make my way out the door, looking around every corner for him. I am scared out of my mind, still seeing flash backs before my eyes. I am totally paranoid. I jump into my car frantically trying to lock the doors. I am in total panic mode and this crazy picture show is now flashing in my face, and I am not sure what is real and what is memory. I drive. I almost hit 3 cars, tears running down my face; I make it to my boyfriend's house. I knock on the door, and he is surprised to see me. I drop into his arms and weep. He has not a clue about what had happened to me in regards to Jerry, and he has limited information about what my mother did to me. I totally freaked him out by showing up there hysterical. He had no clue with what I was about to hit him with. MY PAST!

He held me while I cried, and when I was able to speak again. I told him about Jerry, and what he did to me. I did not go into the details, but I told him how he would hit me and rape me. I then went on to tell him how my family knew and nobody did anything about it. I explained how my mother would torture me, and I had to admit to him that I had an abortion. I was terrified to let those words flow from my mouth. I never admitted that to anyone before. I felt if I told him, he would hate me. He thought I was a virgin, and I'd lied. I was so embarrassed, and felt so dirty about all of it. I was ashamed of it, but I knew I had to tell him before it traveled all over school when we went back.

When it was over, and I had told him, he held me tight and said, "It is ok, Lisa, it was not your fault, and I still love you." I just lay there silently for a long time.

I was surprised; he did not look at me any differently, and was very understanding.

I just hit him with a bomb, but he remained calm and caring. This was not the reaction I expected, and I was overwhelmed that he could care that much about me. I respected him so much for just loving me.

Summer was now over and it was off to high school to face my demons. I was ready to take on senior year.

☙ CHANGING SEASONS ❧

The tides are changing for this beautiful
Young girl, a tornado has landed emotions
Up in a whirl...

With the change of the seasons, and for
All time, this young girl it testing out
A new rhyme...

Once angry and bitter like the perfect
Storm brewing, now calm and light, like
The newly fallen snow, shining bright
In the moonlight with a special glow...

What a transformation right in front
Of my eyes, like the fall leaves shining
So bright... Filled with color upon color
Where does it end, filled with life, new
Emotion, a strange new world she Began...

Hard work and effort has brought her
Here, knowing her family was always Near...

Excepting change, learning to let go
Like the tides of freedom let the winds Blow...

Pushing her forward let the tornado
Pass, like Dorothy and the wizard, she
Came down in a crash...

The magic of reality one scary blow,
Time to move forward start a brand
New show...

CHAPTER 11
Winds of Time

Chapter 11

Winds of Time

Taking on Senior Year

After I let Mark know what had happened to me, I felt a sense of relief. I didn't have to hide it from him anymore, and I could let my guard down. He had proved to me that he was the good guy that I always knew that he would be, and my trust level was through the roof. I felt like I had grown up so much in that moment after I had told him. I know I did not tell him everything, but I did tell him what I was capable of letting out at that time in my life, and it was big for me. It was another step I was taking towards moving forward in my life, and I was trying to put the evil past behind me.

I went back to school with my head held high and my spirits intact. I knew the stories would be swirling around, and I was ready to face them head on. It didn't take

Long for people to start whispering again, and of course there are always the bold ones that come right up to you, and BAM in your face with questions. I used to call them the nosey ones. The kids in high school that had to know everything—they needed up to the minute reports of all the high school drama.

This time around I was smarter, a little more mature, and I stayed cool as a cucumber when I was hit with questions. I did not go into detail, but I explained briefly that it was all lies. I still refused to admit to having an abortion. The fact that it happened affected me greatly, and I felt an extreme sense of guilt over it. Mark agreed not to tell a soul about it, and he stood by me 100%. It really was nobody's business, and at one point I just started saying, "I am not even going to answer your questions, as it is none of your business." I received a lot of criticism for it, and of course the skeptics stated that since I wasn't talking it must be true. I didn't care what anyone thought, and I stood strong, but it just would not go away.

I was trying to ignore it, but the girlfriend wouldn't let it go, and Jerry was fueling her. I know he was trying to get to me, break me down again, but I would not let him in. I was not that little girl anymore, vulnerable, scared, and helpless. I was maturing into a strong, fearless young woman who was not going to let anyone put me down again. I was not going to ever let anyone ever control me again. I could have fought this girl many times, as we had many words, but I actually felt sorry for her, because I knew what he was doing to her. I would say to her when she would taunt me, "I know the real him, and he has you so controlled you need to run fast, and reclaim your life." She hated when I would say stuff like that, and she would just call me a whore. I wanted to hit her desperately, beat the shit out of her, and I didn't because I knew that is what he wanted. It took a lot of self control not to bop her in the face. I knew I was slowly winning the fight, because I would not give in to his games. The harder they pushed, I pushed right back! This time I was not going to let him get the upper hand. I know this infuriated him as he needed total control at all times. I was trying to think like him, to out smart him. I was trying to remain strong and confident.

I guess I must have angered him enough, because he started showing up at the school, and was talking about me to anyone that would listen.

I was definitely intimidated by him, because when I saw him in the parking lot I would run the other way. Yes, here I am again running, how sad. It made me feel so worthless again. I started struggling with those old feelings, and I had hidden depression over it. So I mentally squashed it. I buried it deep deep inside my head, and heart. I never wanted to talk of any of it again, so that is what I did. I ignored my feelings, and pressed on. I fought so hard for myself on every level of my life.

One day it all came to a head. Jerry went over the top and showed up at my place of work with her to harass me. I felt so sick. Looking him square in the eyes. His evil glare, and pompous smile, he was so smug. I wanted to pound him in the face until he died right in front of me. He was rubbing her arm and looking at me like he wanted a piece of me right there. It reminded me of the moment at his house with his niece when he raped me in front of her, then touched her all over. I was so sick to my stomach looking at him, and I was getting an instant flash back to that moment so long ago. I didn't know what to do, so I was silent, still varying between past and present. He started yelling obscene things at me, and she was laughing I could hear her laugh echoing so loud in my ears. I just wanted it to stop. A good friend of mine worked with me. She came over next to me, and told him to leave immediately. He walked out the door-yelling whore over and over again. One single tear dripped from my eye, and my friend said, "What was that all about? Are you alright?" I told her I was, and turned and went back to work not speaking of it again until I saw my boyfriend. Well, he had had enough of all of it. The next day he went and tracked Jerry down. He was staying at this apartment complex with his girlfriend, and her family. Some of our friends lived there as well, and would see him all the time. We went together, and met up with our friends. Mark spotted Jerry, and of course the coward started running. My boyfriend chased him down and proceeded to beat the shit out of him in front of a big group of people. He then forced Jerry to publicly apologize to me for all the lies he had been saying about me. I was shocked that Jerry admitted to lying and said he was sorry out loud for all to hear. I looked at him, and realized what a true coward he really was. He could prey on me as a defenseless kid, or his young niece, but to another guy he would say anything to save himself from a beating. I saw the real him for the first time. He was the one who was begging for his life now, and he was just a scared little boy at that moment crying in front of all of us. I realized right then and there that he must have been abused by someone as a child. He unleashed all his anger and repressed feelings onto me, because someone tortured him. All of these thoughts were rushing through my head as all of this was unfolding before my eyes. I actually felt pity for him, but I knew he needed that beating and deserved it. I yelled to my boyfriend to stop, and let him go. "Please let this be over," I said. I looked Jerry in the eyes standing strong, and said it again loud and clear. He looked at me and said, "OK Lisa, it's over!" I turned and walked away. I did not want to ever look at him again. I wanted to get on with my life and leave all the evil right there in that moment forever. I prayed as I walked away that it would not follow me any more.

After that day, the stories finally started to die down. He did not come to the school anymore, and she left me alone. I would see her walk by in school with black eyes all the time, and bruises. I felt bad. I tried to warn her, but she would not listen to me. I had to save myself at this point, but every time I saw her, my heart would break for her, and I would say a little prayer that she would be ok, and leave him one day. When she became pregnant, she dropped out of school before we graduated. I never saw her or him again. I heard through the grapevine that they had a little girl. Once in a while I would wonder, would he go on to sexually abuse his child/children. The thought sickened me to the core and I just blocked in out and moved forward with my life.

This was another transition period for me. I left it all there on that day. I did not talk about it anymore. I could not handle talking about it anymore. If I went back to it, it would have consumed me, and I would of fallen apart. I refused to fall apart, and be like my mother. She was still up to the same old tricks, and I road the roller coaster of her insane world every day of my life. I was still running. I was never home, and spoke to her as little as possible. When we did talk it was either, a senseless conversation, or a vicious argument. I hated her. I blamed her for everything. I was embarrassed of her, and I loathed her for all that she represented. So I created my own world. It consisted of school, work, more work and my boyfriend. That is how I survived senior year.

I did make some new friends along the way, and went out and had some fun for myself. I re-established my friendship with Allie after a year, and I was happy not to have that weighing on my head anymore. Things were moving along now. I was babysitting my sister every weekend, as my dad was a bartender on the weekends and Karen would go sit with him. I didn't mind, I enjoyed taking care of her, and Mark would come with me. We had a lot of fun the three of us. I felt content with a lot of the things that were going on in my life. I was also thinking about my future, and college. I wanted to go to art school. My art teacher was pushing me to go. He said I had enough talent to make it. I really wanted to pursue that dream, but I did not want to go to school for four years. I wanted to do something quick so I could start making good money, and move out. That was my goal, getting out of that house for good. After much thought, I gave up on my dream to be an artist, and decided to go to a business college instead. I enrolled in a one-year secretarial course, and applied for financial aid. My art teacher was disappointed, and continued to try to change my mind, but my decision was made and I stuck with it. I could not wait to graduate and move on.

It was now getting closer to prom and graduation. As my boyfriend was a year younger than me, and a junior, I went to two proms that year. Two of my friends were dating younger guys as well, so we all went to junior prom together. Then it was off to senior prom together again. We had a blast at both proms. So many great memories were made for sure. We all looked fabulous for the time, you know it was the 80s, so poofy-sleeved dresses and lots of lace. The guys in different colored tuxedos with matching tie cumberbun and shoes. The colors were great! It went from white, to light blue, and burgundy. The ruffled men's shirts were the best with the colored string on the tip of the ruffles to match the tuxedo. The 80s were truly a magical time for sure. With two proms out of the way it was onto the picnics.

The next day was senior picnic day. Mark and I had planned to go, but his mother had other plans for us. His sister was a senior, and could not find a date to the prom, so I extended myself and found one for her. It was not the guy she wanted to go with, but he was a really nice person. I figured as long as she had a date she could be there and enjoy the night like the rest of us. The guy she wanted to go with had no interest in her, and had a date already. I tried to explain that to her the best I could without hurting her feelings. She was a little sheltered and quite spoiled. She was hearing impaired, and did not have many friends. People were not kind to her, so she was angry. She just wanted to fit in like the rest of us, and I thought by going with someone as a friend might help. I always extended myself to her all the time. I did like her a lot, but she was hard to get along with, but I always tried. Well, I talked one of my friends into asking her, and he did. What does she do she says NO! I was so angry with her. I told her I was angry, and felt that she had an opportunity and she blew it. She said he wasn't good enough for her, and she refused to go with him. I was like, "Well, the guy you want to go with hasn't even looked your way twice, so why not just go as friends!" She still refused. I was embarrassed as I told this guy she would definitely go, my mistake. Well, I didn't even want to talk to her after that. I felt she blew an opportunity to branch out, meet new people, and have some fun! My friend found another date, and he was able to enjoy that evening, which made me feel good because after that fiasco, I was worried he would not go.

So senior prom came, it was awesome and she sat home and sulked. The next day I went to Mark's house to pick him up for the picnic. The car was packed with food, drinks, and our bathing suits everything we would need to have a great day. At least 100 kids were going. I go inside, and he proceeds to tell me that since we are not bringing his sister to the picnic his mother said we couldn't go. I was like wait a minute, where did this "WE STUFF" come into it. She is not my mother, and she cannot tell me what to do! She asked me to find her daughter a date, and I did. It was not my fault that she wouldn't go! I did not want to take his sister because I was pissed at her for embarrassing me, and I didn't want to deal with her crap all day. I wanted to have fun. I told him, I was going with or without him. He said, "Lisa, I am not going, my mom said NO and that is it!" Then I said, "This is crap, let's just go!" He said NO, and I shouldn't go without him, it's not right.

I am a senior, this is my picnic, I want to go so bad I am pissed, but I stay home with him because he is mad that I wanted to go without him. We spent the day at his house, helping them do yard work, as his sister sat inside watching TV. His mother was thrilled we were there, as it was what she wanted. I was pissed off as hell and ignored everyone. This is the moment our relationship started to unwind. I was pissed that he did not have a backbone to stand up to his mother. His father didn't care if we went; she was just trying to control everything. That word, "control," it makes me crazy, even to this day! The thought of being controlled in any way puts me over the top. Oh, I told him exactly how I was feeling about it, and he was so mad at me for speaking poorly about his mother. I didn't care. I went home that day, thinking I am not going to be controlled by this woman ever again.

Graduation Day

Finally Graduation day was here. I was so excited. I accomplished something great. I graduated with Honors. I was accepted into the business school, and received a grant to help me through. I was so proud of myself. I will finally be able to leave my past there, and embark on new adventures, where people will not know me. I do not have to explain myself to anyone. They will only know the parts of me that I choose to let them know. I felt on top of the world. I felt like I was truly growing up.

Of course my graduation day had its ups and downs. My mother decided to created chaos at the house before I left, which was no surprise to me. Shouting at me, about how if I decide to leave her she will rip all my hair out of my head and stab me in the eye. Now that is an interesting thing to say to your daughter on her graduation day! Congratulations and I am proud of you would have been so much better.

It did not surprise me, that my mother would do something to turn it around, and make it about her. That is what she did best. She wanted all the attention and sympathy all the time. In a way it was like she had Munchausen Syndrome, but on a psychotic level. That is the best way that I can describe it. It was always about her suffering, her life, her feelings, and the pathetic analogies of all who wronged her and my brother.

I was determined to enjoy my day, and not let her ruin it. I left the house feeling proud and confident, and my family brought my mother. They were in charge of keeping her under control, as this was my day to shine NOT hers! I was worried because my father was going to be there, as well as my grandmother and aunt. I didn't want my mother going up to them and cause a scene. I told family members beforehand to please just for this one day help, and they did. I said if she acts up take her home!

Graduation was about to start all the kids were lining up and my dad was still not there. I could hear the band starting to play, as they were warming up, and still no dad. I refused to get in line, as I was pacing back and forth looking, searching for him in the crowd. I was so upset. I was thinking how could he miss this. My mind started racing, and my stomach was churning. I was going into an anxiety attack, I was ready to blow and then I saw him. For a brief moment I was feeling instantly better until I got a closer look. He had on his sunglasses and he was pale. I knew that look—he was hung over. My grandmother and aunt were in tow behind him, and both were extremely angry. He hugged and kissed me. He smelled like stale alcohol and cigarettes. At that moment, I didn't even care, I was just glad he was there. My aunt took a couple of quick pictures. He told me he loved me and was very proud of me. I told him where my mother was sitting so he could stay far away, and off I went with my friends to graduate. The music was now playing very loud, and I was running to find my place in line. It was all a blur after that, and it went by in an instant. Next thing I know everyone was in the audience were clapping, students were throwing their hats up in the air and hugging. My friends and I were jumping up and down, laughing and cheering. What a great moment in time. One I will never forget. When the ceremony was over, that was my dad's cue to leave, and he left quickly. He did not want to run into my mother, so I didn't even get to say good-bye. Of course my mother tracked me down, and I made that experience as brief as possible. I told her I would be home soon. They were having a little party for me, which was very nice.

My family got together on a positive note for a change and I was actually very

happy to spend time with them. I was even kind to my mother, as I was thankful for all the hard work she did to put it all together.

That night all the seniors were getting together in the school parking lot to celebrate. It was a High School tradition that went on for years, and we planned on making history repeat itself for another year. The police were there for crowd control, but they left us alone to dance, and party the night away! It was truly epic.

I leave my party, and head over to pick up Mark so we could meet up with everyone at the school. I show up, and he looks at me and says, "If we cannot take my sister I cannot go." I was like whatever, I was not missing this, so we will take her. She graduated too, so it was the right thing to do. Then he says that he had a 10 p.m. curfew. He never had a curfew before, so I looked at him and said, "Ok, then I will drop you and your sister back off, and I am going back to be with my friends." I was not going to let his mother control me, and that is what I did. I brought them home on time, and he went into the house with his tail between his legs, and I just pulled away. He was so angry with me, but I explained to him I am doing my own thing, and if he wanted to be a mamma's boy then that was his choice. I was not going to listen to her, why should I? I take care of myself—always have and always will.

I parted ways with all my friends from high school, and many of them I never saw again. Most of my close friends were traveling and partying all summer before going to college in the fall. I chose a more mature path. I was motivated to move out. I had a plan and wanted to start as soon as possible. I chose to start college two weeks after my graduation. While all my friends partied and truly enjoyed their last moments of being carefree teens, I was studying hard, and was working hard. I felt I needed to keep pushing forward, no time to stop, no time to rest. I had to keep on moving. It was ok, because I was not a normal teen anyways. My life path changed a long time ago, and I was never granted the privilege of just being a kid.

꧁ WINDS OF TIME ꧂

Secret emptiness of her quiet being…

Who is this beauty before me?

This delicate flower looking to be set
Free into a field of dreams where she can
Prosper peacefully…

Sun rise, sun set on a perfect spring
Day where the wind blows with whispers of
A painful past.

A story untold – silent like the stillness before
A storm brewing inside the core of this breakable
Flower trying to grow, survive the changing
Seasons. Making it through the storm.

Winter so cold like a heart frozen in time, hibernating to
Protect oneself from the world around her…

Waiting for the right climate to come forward
Into the light and shine so bright!

Story unfolding through the winds of time,
Chiming in ones ear, louder for all to hear…

What is she trying to say, actions pulling her
Far away, wanting to make it, survive the storm,
Looking for summer to keep her warm…

As the brisk air comes on in she is letting go
Of her personal sins, shedding the scars that have
Held her down, keeping her buried in the ground...

Grateful for the gentle breeze, a loving hug
A tight squeeze... Saving her from that cold winters
Night, guiding her to the light...

Bumps and bruises along the way a survivor she
Is here to stay...

CHAPTER 12

My Mother Part 1: Arms of Sorrow

Chapter 12

My Mother Part 1 : Arms Of Sorrow

When I think of my mother many things come to mind, but the word that I feel fits best is courageous. I am sure you are thinking WOW that is not what I was thinking of, as you can say she was crazy, out of control, mean spirited, even EVIL.

I say courageous because I do believe we all have a life plan that we are given before we even reach this earthly plain. I know everyone has different beliefs about life, death and religion, but this is my personal belief. So as you read all of this, take it for what it is my thoughts and views. This is not my way of preaching to anyone at all. I am just processing all that I have been through with my mom.

Joann chose to suffer. Her soul chose a life of suffering, I believe as a learning lesson. Our souls come to this earth to learn and evolve, and I feel we all have different levels that we need to achieve to enrich us in the afterlife. The question I have is Why Me? Why was I chosen to be her daughter, and have to endure the incredible pain and suffering at the hands of a mother who is mentally ill?

Maybe she chose me so I can reach my destiny of what I am supposed to achieve in this lifetime, or maybe it was because she felt that she could trust that I would stay by her side, no matter how tough it becomes, or how horrible she is. I have suffered at the hands of this woman for years, and I still feel committed to her. I still love her, and I will never abandon her. My mother has been pushed to the wayside by her husband, who left her alone sick to care for a young child. Her family who has basically disowned her because of her illness, and many of her so-called friends did as well. This woman has suffered beyond belief, and her words ring in my ear like a disturbing melody filled with hope and dread. Her words, " I CHOOSE LIFE," "I STILL HAVE WORK TO DO HERE ON THIS EARTH." These words haunt me, because it is hard being her daughter. It is hard to continue to endure this emotional torture that she projects onto me, and now seeping onto my innocent family who never signed up for this mess, or did they?

My Mom, The Beginning...

To give you some basic background information about my mother will help you understand where it all began. I will not get into crazy detail just a brief overview of her younger years. I feel it will give you a better picture of where the problems started, and the signs that were missed along the way.

My mom was the oldest of four children. Born into an Italian family. Her father was an incredible man with a heart of gold, but he was a heavy drinker and a gambler. He had jet-black thick hair, was dark skinned, and looked like Dean Martin. He worked very hard to provide for his family, but his shortcomings caused a lot of grief on the home front. There was a lot of tension and fighting.

Her mother was a very strong spirited woman, quite intelligent, but going blind. She was absolutely beautiful with a round face and broad smile. She always kept herself just so, with her hair done up everyday. She enjoyed looking good, a very well put together woman. She got her business sense from her father, who owned several apartment buildings. My grandmother would help her father take care of business, and she was extremely savvy for that time period. Her biggest struggle was her on-coming blindness, and my grandfather's wicked ways.

They didn't have a lot of money, and they lived a very modest lifestyle. They lived in an Old Italian neighborhood in New Haven, CT. It was a six family house owned by her grandfather. My aunt was born after my mother, they were very close in age and the boys came later on. My mother was a very different kind of child. She was nervous and anxious all of the time. She was always scared and paranoid. These emotions and fears overflowed onto my aunt. They shared a bedroom together and my mother always did outrageous things. For example, my mom would pinch my aunt at night while she was sleeping in her bed waking her up and scaring her. My aunt was frightened and traumatized by her, as my mom would always do things to her (you see the pattern.) She would also say crazy things like, "I need to sleep without covers and be cold to sacrifice for our grandmother's blindness. " What child does these sorts of things? Even as a child, she would choose to suffer!

So you see at a young age my mother was a sick girl. My mom also took care of HER blind grandmother. She would go to her house and sit with her and care for her after school. That started when she was around 8 years old. As other children were out playing and having fun, she was cleaning and watching her grandmother. She always felt stressed, and cried a lot. She spoke of looking out the window watching the other children playing and was upset that she could not be out there with them. I am sure the emotional aspect of taking care of others at such a young age chipped away at her nervous system as she was already having issues. Her psyche was fragile for sure.

On a good note, when my mom talks about this time period in her life, she states that her grandmother paid her a quarter every week and she gave her a jar to put it in. My mother, with a smile on her face, reminisced about how she was able to save her money and go to the store to buy penny candy for herself and her sister. Even through the painful memories of her past, she always would come up with great stories that made her happy. She had great moments in her life that made her strong and resilient. These memories encouraged her to continue on even through her mania and pain. When she was at her best, she always looked to the positive things in life. She always looked to share her wisdom with others. Even though she was a sick woman, she had a kind heart.

Joann was demanding as a child, and always got her way. She would have big explosions and meltdowns until she got what she wanted. She was a bully. These sets of behaviors followed her throughout her adult years. I witnessed her on many, many occasions having a tantrum when things didn't turn out as she wanted. Imagine this grown woman acting like a small child when she couldn't get her own way. It was sad to watch and extremely frustrating.

Unfortunately, she was molested at the hands of her grandfather (my grandfather's father). She also had a local storeowner expose himself to her, which traumatized her even further. At this time in her life the family moved to West Haven. As a young teen she was so nervous and guilt riddled. She had low self-esteem and never thought of herself as pretty or smart. Which was not the case at all. She was drop dead gorgeous with brains to boot, she just didn't know it!

She met my dad at 13 years old and they started dating. Right from the beginning, they fought all the time. He was always jealous and she was a basket case. They grew up together, they learned how to smoke together and decided to get married even though they were battling constantly. They broke up several times, but they were always drawn to each other. I never understood this, as they never had any communication what so ever! Bottom line is that they loved each other. Love can be so blind sometimes, and in their case it was a fact. I also believe that they were meant to be together, and that they were soul mates. If they never became a couple, my brother and I would have never been. Life...

My mother became a wonderful hairdresser and my dad a grocery store manager.

They bought a house, and decided to start a family. My mother was terrified to have children, and when she looked back on the experience she told me how she had the baby blues (as they called it back in the day), and was totally depressed.

Shortly, thereafter my brother was born, and then me. We lived in a beautiful house, in a wonderful neighborhood. From the outside looking in we were the perfect family unit. Now that observation was far from the truth. My dad worked all the time, as he was a true workaholic, and strived on having material things and the best of everything. My mom on the other hand was falling apart. She stopped working to care for us, and only took care of certain customers in our home.

She was always crying and smoking, as she was extremely depressed. I remember her as young as 2, sitting crying, talking, and smoking. My brother and I would just play on the floor near her, and she was oblivious of our presence most of the time. She would be deep in thought, and seemed to be off in never never land.

Again, when she looks back and talks about these moments, she states that some of her best memories of us as kids where when we would sit on the floor playing together and she could just watch. I thought that she was totally oblivious to what we were doing, but she shared with me that this was not the case. There were times when she actually was fully connected. I guess as children we could not tell the difference, as they were so far and few between.

Finally, she just had a complete breakdown. She went off to the hospital, and my brother and I went to my grandma Rose's house. She was starting to really go blind at this point but she managed to care for us, as I stated before she was a very strong woman, with deep virtues. My grandmother was tough as nails, and I think I get some of my toughness from her.

My mom was gone for four months, as she did not want to come home. She felt she could not handle taking care of us. We stayed with my grandmother, and my dad would come visit. When my mom finally got out of the hospital we all stayed at my grandparents house, until my mom was ready for us to go home.

We finally made it home, but she was a zombie half of the time. I used to sit and watch her, and think to myself, (I was maybe 4 years old at this point) wondering what was wrong with her, she acted so strange all the time. I got a very weird vibe from her, and she scared me a lot of times. I couldn't quite grasp why my mother would come and go the way she did. I was only 4, so I didn't understand what was happening to her, but I was aware of the changes. I was extremely sensitive to it, so it affected me greatly.

Then the unthinkable happened, my brother got sick with Leukemia, and that sent her into a tailspin, as it would for any loving parent, but for her so much worse because she was mentally ill. She had little support. My dad was a rough man, and frowned upon her illness, and hated the fact that she took medicine for it. He would down her all the time, and was verbally abusive to her. When she gained weight due to her medications, he called her fat.

So, my brother is sick, she is trying to cope, and she and my dad have zero communication. One can imagine how horrible this was. On top of it all I was in the middle of all this madness. Witnessing everything. At this point I was 5 yrs old and starting kindergarten. I was a very insecure child. I cried a lot at school and wet my pants on more than one occasion. I loved my brother dearly and could not grasp what was going on with him, or my family. All I knew is that he was sick, and my parents were sad and angry all the time.

After two long years he lost his battle to Leukemia at the age of 9, and I was 6. This began a new chapter of my mother's mania at a more intense level. On the home front, my house was a living nightmare filled with either silence, or rage depending on the moment.

At this point my dad was gone all the time, and when he was home all they did was fight. I was left with my mother alone most of the time, and sometimes it was quite terrifying. Some nights I would wake up from a sound sleep to find her standing next to my bed just staring at me, with this blank lifeless look about her. I would say, Mommy, what are you doing, and she would not respond just stare. I would cry sometimes, terrified but she would just walk away. Other nights I would hear music and banging. I would get up and my mother would be rearranging the house, taking things off the walls, hammering, cleaning, and even painting at 2 a.m. It was bizarre and maddening at the same time, the crazy look in her eyes as she was on overdrive.

Then there would be the nights that she and my dad would fight. They would be so vicious with each other, verbally attacking one another. My dad would get so enraged that he would throw things and break things. My mom would snarl at him, and say mean things to trigger him even more. He would break everything around her, and she would sit there smoking her cigarettes taunting him, until he would either leave or just go to bed. The nights that he was drunk he would end up in my room, as I wrote earlier on and pass out at the end of my bed asking me if I love my daddy!

All this chaos went on over the next few years, and my mom did a couple more stints in the hospital, and I would go to my grandparent's house until she was calm again. As I was getting older, I was overly aware of her behaviors, and watched her change in a moments notice. She would be a zombie, then she would be high as a kite (manic), and then sobbing and depressed. It was a roller coaster ride that I could not get off of. My mom would dance around the kitchen singing and peeing all over her self laughing uncontrollably. Pee was all over the floor, and she didn't care she would just keep on dancing. She even did this in front of my friends, and it was quite embarrassing.

She would randomly show up at the school playground sometimes just to check on me. I would see her drive up in her little brown Mustang, smoking and yelling out the window to get my attention. I would just want to die. I was in 5th grade at this point, and quite embarrassed of my mother. I would get teased all the time, and it infuriated me to no end. My mother didn't care, she would follow the bus to make sure I got to school ok, and even came into the school with my dog running down the hallway because she had a bad feeling something was wrong. It was endless. Day in and day out something was always happening.

On the down days she would just sit for hours and cry. Talking to her self, cursing God, waving her fist in the air, screaming for my brother. At these times, it was so disturbing for me, and I had nobody to talk to about it. I would pretend it was not real. I would go out the door in the morning go to school, and pretend everything was great. Inside I was tormented. I did not know how to verbally express what I was feeling. I just sucked it up and went on with my days, taking the good with the bad.

When my dad finally had enough and left us, that is when the bad went to worse. My mom stopped taking her medicine, and was full out crazy. This is when the verbal and physical abuse started with me. She turned on me, and like a switch it was on.

I will not repeat myself as to the issues with Jerry, as I already discussed it, but I want to give you a full-blown picture of the abuse I took at the hands of my mother at her worse state. She was unforgiving. She would yell at me all the time, and tell me she was going to stab me.

I had long, long hair and she would come to my bed at night with a scissors and threaten to cut all my hair off. Other times she would stand there with a knife, and just look at me, with these cold black eyes piercing through me. I was frozen with fear, and I would try to communicate with her, but she would not answer. She would just mumble and walk away. I literally slept with one eye open so to speak, when I slept at all.

My mom's behavior was so erratic. She would drive down the road, hit cars, and leave. I remember one time she rear-ended a car, the guy gets out of his car, and comes to the window yelling at her. She rolls down her window tells him to go fuck himself and backs up and drives away. The cops showed up at our house, and it was a big mess. After that she would have me drive all the time because she just didn't feel like it anymore. I was 12 when I started driving. I went everywhere. The only time she drove was when she went to work, other than that it was on me.

I will never forget another day when my mom showed up at school. I was in middle school at this point, and my mom came in with a see-through nightgown on with nothing underneath. She waltzed in, and was screaming for me. Everyone was laughing, the principal approached her trying to get her out, and she was screaming for me over and over. I came around the corner as I heard her, and when I saw all the commotion I ran for my life. I was mortified. My mom standing there, you could see everything, it was horrible. The principal finally got her to leave and called my dad. The next day I was called to the office to talk about it, but nothing further ever came of it after that. She was told she was not allowed at the school anymore, and that was the end of that. They never called social services to report it. They wanted to push it under the carpet. What a disservice to me!

I was tormented and teased unmercifully at this point, and I was angry as hell. My mother was always doing things like that to me. Countless acts of embarrassment, over and over again.

She would also invite young boys from school to my house, and other wayward kids that I didn't like. They were trouble. She always had kids in our home, and they started saying in school that they were having sex with my mother. I honestly do not know what happened, but one young man had some type of experience with my mother, and bragged about it saying he was sleeping with her. I never saw it so I am not sure what really happened, but all the same the embarrassment was endless.

One evening I was out with my aunt, we went to the movies. On returning home that evening she walked me in. I come inside and the heat was up to 85 degrees the house was hot as hell. I look over and she is sitting there smoking with these crazy eyes not speaking. I go over and turn the heat down, and all of a sudden she jumps off the couch like a maniac screaming, and she attacks me for turning the heat down. I run into the kitchen and she catches me, then she grabs a meat tenderizer and beats me with it over and over again. I am covering my head as she has me blocked into a corner! My aunt was speechless and shocked, but then she started yelling at my mother to stop, and that is when my mother turned on her. She rushed forward like a freight train, hands stretched straight out and took her nails then dug them into my aunt's face and scratched her all up. My mother was pushing her and my aunt fell out the door. My mother slammed the door shut spewing obscenities at her, than proceeds to beat the shit out of me. I was finally able to get away from her, and I locked myself in the bathroom.

About 20 minutes later my dad showed up. My aunt called him. He comes in, and I think to myself, thank God I will be saved, but NO he yells at my mother, briefly talks to me and leaves. I am like that is it! Leave me here! I was baffled. This was one of the many times when I thought I was going to be saved, but sadly disappointed. Those marks stayed on my back for a month, a constant reminder of that horrible evening every time I looked in the mirror.

My uncle (my mom's younger brother) came to see us after that incident and sat and talked to me. I told him what happened, and I did say to him I think we need help. He said to me, "What do you want me to do about it!" I remember this moment clearly sitting on my bed, looking to him for some help, and him blowing me off. I had deep resentment towards him for years after that one statement. I think now, why was I so angry with him for so many years? Then I realized the answer. He was the first person I was able to outwardly express my fear and desperateness to, only to be shot down and ignored. That is why the silence for me continued. Nobody listened!

I spent a lot of time being angry and resentful towards my family. I would think why did they leave me here with her? Am I not worth saving? I would ponder these things over and over again feeling betrayed by all the people who where supposed to love me! There were a lot of people around that knew what was happening, and not ONE person would step forward to help. Honesty, to this day I still do not get it. I have asked a few family members why, but not one could give me a definitive answer that makes sense. They did express to me, that back in that time frame, it was up to the father to take charge of a situation like that, and others did not over step there boundaries! My question was, when the father does not step up, what happens next? I never got an answer that satisfied me! All I know is if the shoe were on the other foot, I know in my heart that I would come forward to help someone in need, especially family. I guess I think quite differently from them.

I know I am writing this in the middle of my story, but I feel that I need to express this to you, as thinking back to this memory brings me to an old place in my mind and heart that was so broken.

I was so disappointed in my family, and the hurt was endless. I can still picture sitting on that bed hearing those words of rejection, seeing my room feeling defenseless, helpless;, once again alone. Lost in the madness of my life, twisted and distorted like Alice in Wonderland with a pure shot of evil…

So the story goes on…

At this point in time, she made it a regular thing to beat the crap out of me for no apparent reason. I would walk in the door, and never knew what to expect. One moment it was I love you so much my beautiful daughter and the next it was I want to stab you, kill you, or she would just beat me up. She would tell me she was the best mother in the world and I was blessed to have her. I would just look at her with such hatred, and wished her dead on countless occasions.

In the morning I would eat my breakfast and she would throw forks or knives at me. I would dodge silverware all the time, as it was an everyday occasion. This was our ritual, and it became a game of cat and mouse for us. The big joke was she broke all her silverware throwing them at me. I got really good at dodging them, and that made her so mad! I relished in the fact that there was something I could outsmart her with. I took great pleasure in pissing her off! Sounds corny, but this was my little revenge. This was something I actually had control of, and I believe that is why I was so good at it. My life was hell, between the abuse from my mother, plus Jerry, and the absence of my dad, I was just out of my mind.

When she didn't come home on the fateful day, and I got to leave that house for the last time, I had a glimmer of hope that things would be different. I felt maybe just maybe I had a chance at surviving all of this madness. As we drove away from the house of hell, I thanked God and my brother for hearing my cries for help.

Funny thing… As we waited to find my mom, I had all these secret thoughts

And fantasies…

In a child's mind, I thought maybe she would be better now and I would have the mom that I always wanted. Now that we were getting out of this house, I thought she would come back to love me and take care of me finally like it should be. My child like visions of a mom who nurtured me, loved me, and made me feel special like all children long for. This beautiful daydream that I would continually have, hoping for it to be a reality!

I was secretly hoping and praying to God that my mom would return and be this wonder woman swooping in to save me from this nightmare that no child should ever have to experience. I wanted the Brady bunch kind of mom, but instead I got one who flew over the cuckoo's nest!

When she finally returned home the next day, all of my hopes of her being better, my dreams, destroyed right in front of my eyes as she walked through the door!

My fairy tale mom was just the glimmer of hope in the eyes of a young girl yearning for a better life, yearning for a healthy mom.

Sad to say that day never came…

ARMS OF SORROW

There are days when I am tired and weak... On
Those days in the arms of sorrow I seek...

Sometimes, life to hard to bear, drowning in the
Dark waters of despair... Waters beating down on me so
Hard... This never-ending rain pounding, burning, so scarred...

Pulled into the abyss... Funneling deep into the depths
Of the ocean floor... Down so far, one cannot see the light of day.
Lungs filled with heavy confliction, thoughts of what life
Is supposed to be, rolled over by waves of open seas...

Why such pain, such confusion?

Thoughts so disturbing, no voice could come through...
Buried in the rubble of a volcano that blew... No
Light coming to guide my way, to find me, save me
Tell me I will be ok...

Seeking refuge in this shipwreck of my mind,
In the arms of sorrow I do find... My comfort, my shelter,
My deep faith, how can one forsake?

When a rush of calming waves barrel over
Me, the warmness of a new day I can finally see...

My personal vessel I do name, "My Shipwreck of Sorrow,"
Sailing off with my pain...

Extended arms, bow so strong... They got me through the wake
Of the storm...

I survived another day, my arms of sorrow showed
Me the way...

Once again, my hope restored, my arms of sorrow
Kept me warm...

I was lost, now I am found my lighthouse
Of hope turned me around... To the safety of land
I do sail! My personal vessel will prevail...

This never-ending faith, a light kept me going through
The worst time of my life!

CHAPTER 13

My Mother Part 2: The Good The Bad and The Ugly: Bi-Polar

Chapter 13

My Mother Part 2: The Good the Bad and the Ugly Bi-Polar

Her Mental Illness:

THE GOOD

My mother, at first glance looks like a wonderful woman with a broad smile on her face and a twinkle in her eyes. Her warmth and kindness shines right through from the essence of her soul. She looks older than her years, as I believe she is an old soul, filled with knowledge and wisdom. She will sit with you and tell you the stories of her life, as she remembers it. She will offers advice to all who are willing to listen. She feels her stories of triumph and tragedies are her lessons she is supposed to teach others.

She always wants to help the lost souls of the world. She has a strong spirit like her mother and a great love of god and religion. She has the kind heart of her father always willing to give until it is all gone. She searches daily for those in need, and offers whatever she can to make it better. It may be a kind word, a story or one of her many crafts. She will knit someone a scarf or a hat, or make a yarn doll, that will bring joy and a smile to your face. She will work endlessly to create paper flowers or tin foil stars, so that she could pass them out on her daily journey of pity. She goes with the seasons like clock work, changing up the items that she makes, from flowers, to bows, to dolls, and stars, she makes sure that she touches as many people as she can to help heal their souls.

Her faith is never ending, and she chooses life at all costs. Her religious heart flows deeply into the depths of her soul, and as she would always say, "My prayers are powerful, and when more than one person prays together it is even better." She was a faithful servant to God, always speaking the good word of the Lord, and encouraging others to do the same. Her belief in the light of God and the angels above helped her to always move forward tirelessly giving of herself to the maximum level. The blessed mother Mary was her go-to girl in times of need and trouble. She called out to Mary countless times, and always felt she received the answers she was looking for. This woman of faith could never be wavered. She had a strong will and a strong heart.

As for family, they are number one in her life, and she loves each and every one of them with every ounce of her being. Her love for each person was very personal and unique. She had a reason for everything she did, and in her heart she always felt she was doing the right thing. She will pray the rosary daily for our safety and well-being. She will do continual novenas for our successes in this world. She prays ever day, sometimes all day so her family will be ok. This is her way of protecting us. She always felt as long as she prayed we would always have her love and guidance.

My mother has very little, but will give above and beyond to help anyone in need. She has even giving away my personal items for the greater good of others. Over the years, many things that I bought her for her own enjoyment went to someone she felt was less fortunate than her. I would get upset with her, as I wanted her to enjoy some things in life, but she always said the same thing to me, "My enjoyment is to see others happy!" She searches for those who are lost and helps them find their way home, wherever that may be. Over the years, I have come to understand my mother's odd ways, and have grown to appreciate the good that she was doing. No matter how small or how large, she always touched someone's heart. I learned a lot of great lessons from her, and my kind heart is definitely a true testament of the legacy she was willing to share.

This is the good part of my mother, the real mom who I know and love. When you look into her heart and see past the wall of shame, and the cobwebs of sorrow, that is where you will find the real light that radiates love and a beautiful soul. That is the true Joann Sega, my beloved mother. She is a true angel of God, a never-ending light.

THE BAD

The words mental illness burns deep into my brain. These words that have branded my mother for life, causing such pain for all who are close enough to see the illness. She is now labeled. In her own words, "I have the name, but they all play the game." She says this all the time, because through her eyes she is normal, and we are all the ones who are crazy. That term, mental illness, this awful disease that has tainted my mother's good soul, and hurt her true spirit. I hate that word, and I despise this illness, as it has robbed me of the mother that could have been. I also have a deep sense of compassion for others out there in this world who are mentally ill, as I have seen first hand what it can do to a person. This double edged sword of emotion bridging between disgust and compassion at the same time. I wonder, was this part of my life lesson?

My description of mental illness…

My mother has the sickness that has crept into her brain changing her from good to bad in a moment's notice. As the chemicals swish around traveling through her thought process, which starts out clear, and end ends up cloudy and delusional. Twisted and distorted, these images float around in her brain. She sees this moving picture show right before her eyes, and plays out the parts as they come forward. She sees a show that nobody else sees!

The lost and distressed mother, the evil villain, or the sultry seductress looking for someone to seduce! Sometimes she becomes the controlling bully wanting everything done her way, and will do anything to get it. Then she turns vile and belligerent wanting to destroy anyone in her path with her hateful words. She is brilliant at every part that she plays, and seems to enjoy the manic high that she feels during the process. She has stated in the past that the rush of mania is a feeling like no other. Once you get a taste of it, you can never get enough of it. It's like a drug addict, the high surpasses everything and everyone.

She goes by the seasons, with times, dates, and months all having a meaning with her ever-changing moods. She has rituals that she does over and over again. Year after year, the exact same thing her repeated patterns that you could guarantee. I could recite the things she says at certain times, as she will repeat it over and over again. I know when she will be up and when she will be down she is like clock work. At times I am sickened by her behavior as I anticipate what is coming next. When she changes she goes from a loving mother to a self-centered bitch, ready to cut your throat if you look at her the wrong way. Oh the seasons, she would call it the great depression!

It is very hard to be a loving daughter to a mentally ill mother. I am always trying to maintain composure. I always have to put my needs aside to take care of hers. I never have a mother to confide in, or share my worries or concerns with. I can never tell her anything that is going on in my world or she will blow it out of proportion and create further chaos. She will always turn every situation around, and claim it as her own demanding sympathy and attention.

I can never do enough for her, and I am never good enough. She insists that I do better! She demands like a spoiled child when she does not get what she wants. It is hard to be faithful to her, and show her love and kindness, when inside I am burning with such hurt and anger. I know this is not my true mother, it is the illness, but it is so parallel that at times it is hard to distinguish the two. My constant struggle throughout my life has been to find balance with the many personalities and emotions that go along with being a child of a mentally-ill mother. A continual struggle has been to learn how to take the good with the bad, and try to appreciate the moments when it is just Joann. I get these brief moments that are incredibly wonderful, and they have to satisfy me until the next time. As she has gotten older, they are father and few between. I am her caretaker, her constant servant. I do what I have to do to make sure her world is safe.

I have been devoted to her since I was 6 yrs old after my brother's death, and I will remain devoted to her until the day she dies. As hard as it is for me, I know it is the right thing to do, and the bottom line is I do love my mother, and want her to be ok. She did not ask for this illness, it just happened.

THE UGLY

When my mother is at her worst, watch out. The not so funny thing about people who are mentally ill is that they randomly believe that they are better, and take themselves off their medications. I have heard countless people with this illness say the same thing, and I am always taken aback when I hear the words, "I am cured!"

Why is this so?

Is it the sick side of the brain trying to convince the person to take themselves off their medications so they can go wild? Are they internally craving the out of control feeling, fully impulsive and totally psycho? Or the feeling of never having to accept responsibility for their actions, and using the CRAZY card to do whatever they feel the need to do? It is like giving permission to be bad! This is how I see it, as I have witnessed it for myself. This illness is tricky and complex. Watching my mother speak straight as an arrow to the appropriate people when she needed to, and when they would walk away, psycho Jo would come out and play... Disturbing...

I have watched my mother do this countless times, and the final result is never a good one. Watching my mother dancing in her own urine laughing so loud and singing on top of her lungs. Arms wailing in the air as if she is doing the alleluia dance shouting, "I am free, I am free! Victory is upon me!"

At times when she is impulsive you never know what or who, you are going to get. One moment she could be quiet and calm, and then switching instantly to anger, as the internal beast arises. I remember watching her sit on the front steps at my grandparent's house smoking and rocking quiet as a church mouse. Then she stood up and started shouting to the neighbors, "Shut the fuck up, niggers, do you hear me shut the fuck up or I will stab you all." Needless to say, they went running into the house with her screaming niggers until they were out of sight. Then just as she was instantly explosive, she was instantly silent again drinking her iced coffee, smoking away with this twisted evil look in her eyes. She would mumble obscenities, eyes glassed over like she was in a trance. Again, she was seeing what nobody else could! At those moments we would leave her alone until she would snap out of it. Then we would hold our breath until the next occasion.

One of the most profound moments for me was when she showed up at school in the see-through nightgown. That image of her standing there in the hall way calling out to me, will stay with me forever. I was mortified, and blown away by her lack of caring for herself and me. She looked so empowered standing there acknowledging that everyone could see her naked body, and she didn't care. She was taking in the moment, and she looked larger than life. That wicked smile on her face as they were escorting her out of the school was daunting. I went through these types of situations countless times growing up and even as an adult today.

Here is one extreme moment never to forget…

One sunny afternoon I received a phone call from a woman who was a manger at the apartment complex where my mother was living at the time. She called to tell me that my mother was lying in the grass with her tube top on and a skirt. She had on NO underwear and was waving her crotch out there for all to see. When the woman approached her, to ask her to stop she yelled at her, "Come suck it!" Needless to say, I told the woman I was on my way, and please do not call the police on her. I begged, as I knew if the police came, she would become violent, and they would have wrestled her to the ground, and possibly hurt her. I have also witnessed this countless times. My mother out of control violent, and being taken away in handcuffs kicking, screaming, and spitting the whole way.

I make my way down to her home, which is an hour away praying the whole time and thinking how much worse can it really get? Well, when I showed up there, and saw her laying in the grass my heart went into my throat, it just got worse!

I approach her and say, "Mom, what the hell are you doing?" Her response, "I am airing out my twat, what are you doing here?" I tell her I was called to get her off the lawn and into some decent clothing. She proceeds to go into a rage, smoking like a crazy woman spiting as she is talking. "Fucking bitches can't take a joke," she spits again and then starts yelling at people going by. "Come on over, and check out my twat, you want a piece? I need a big dick now." I am looking at her, and thinking what the hell am I going to do, because the police will be coming soon if I do not do something now… Profound moment for sure…

Here is the image…

Picture her lying there. She is a heavyset woman, with this extra-small tube top on, brightly colored. I want to say it was yellow as I remember seeing the outline of her breasts and nipples showing through. Her stomach is totally exposed, with this flowing skirt of paisley print (this outfit was one of her favorites during her manic state) jacked up to her waist, no underwear. She is barefoot lying in the grass, smoking her cigarette with vigor. This is my mother. How can this be? Why me? Why her? Why was she cursed with this horrible sickness that overtakes her, and the ending result is this?

I think quickly and start saying all kinds of things to her that might make sense. I was like Mom, you have to get up quick, and go inside or they will call the police. That doesn't work it just makes her more volatile. Then I say, in a stern voice get up now, and lets go inside, your grandchildren would be so embarrassed if they saw you! She looks at me for a moment with one eye closed. I got her attention with that one, and then I quickly follow by saying, what would Jon Jon think? He would not want to see you like this. She pondered for a moment mumbling and grumbling, her intense eyes staring me down, as I hold my breath in silence and wait a moment. Then the explosion…

She is extremely angry and saying all sorts of mean things to me, but she does get up arms waiving in the air, spitting profusely at my feet. I didn't even care, as I was like thank God she is up and moving. We walk inside together, with her telling me what a horrible person I am, and I need to just go die somewhere. At that moment I had wished I could instead of dealing with this shit. As we get up stairs and go into her apartment, she looks at me and says, "Life sucks, and then you die. Lighten up Lisa, you can never take a joke!" I am thinking, a joke? Is this all a joke, a sick joke? I am beside myself.

Once inside, I am a little nervous because I am thinking is she going to attack me once the door is closed. I am not quite sure because she is so manic, and I cannot read her next mood. She is completely impulsive. I remain calm and just sit, trying not to make eye contact right away. I sat with her for a long time that day, and just let her vent. I was silent, just watching. Finally after hours of her yelling she becomes silent. She has finally come down off this insidious high. I offer to make her some food, and she is settled and content. Her eyes are no longer twisted, she looks exhausted, and so am I. We eat together and she seems grateful for the moment. I clean up the mess as she lies on the bed smoking and listening to the radio. As I am cleaning, "Dust In The Wind" comes on and she is singing and now weeping. I feel bad for her in this moment as I can feel her pain as she emotionally mutters the words through her tears. All of her heartache displayed so raw and so true.

It is now time for me to leave. I feel guilty, but my husband and kids are home waiting for me. I hate leaving because I do not know what will happen after I am gone. I say to her, "Mom, promise me you will not go out there like that again." She says, "I can't promise anything." This is a typical response, and one I expected. I then say, "If you continue to do this they will kick you out of here, and you love living here, so please don't." She says, "OK." I go home, worried sick about the next phone call I may get. What will she do next? Every time my phone rings I jump with extreme anxiety of who will be on the other end! It is an awful feeling, always on edge waiting for the next bomb to drop. I am always worried sick about her safety, and the safety of others if they approach her the wrong way. I have seen her attack many people, myself included, for taking the wrong approach. As her daughter it is heartbreaking to witness.

Over the next two days, and after countless phone calls to her doctors and nurses, they agree she is unstable, and needs to be hospitalized. They send an ambulance to pick her up, along with the local police. When they come to get my mother and she realizes what they are going to do she freaks out and is taken out by the police kicking and screaming the whole way. She did for warn them that she will fight tooth and nail to stay home and she even bit an EMT, and got punched in the face by a cop whom she spit on. It was my fear, but I knew deep down inside it was going to happen, as there was no way around it. I knew she would be violent, and would not go out without a fight. My mother without her medications had the strength of ten men!

I go visit her at the hospital, and she is black and blue from head to toe from her altercation. I am sickened by the sight of her all bruised up and beaten down, just sitting there, but I am also painfully aware of what brought her to this very moment. While I am visiting, she proceeds to tell me that in the next room they are sexually abusing the children and I need to stop it. I tell her that the children are fine. She says, "NO, look through that window," and she points to an empty wall. I say what window, "Mom? She points again and says look. I see all the children in there, and they are crying. Then she screams, "They are being abused by all the bad men over and over again, and I cannot help them." She will not stop screaming and crying so I tell her, "Don't worry Mom, I will save the children, please just take care of you." In the moment lying to her was the only way to calm her down. She drops onto the floor puts her hands together and starts praying out loud to Mary. Hail Mary Full of Grace, Maria! Maria! She is screaming in Italian tears flowing from her eyes, as she is sobbing, and praying at the same time. As I stand there watching my heart breaks for her.

I go to her and kiss her on the top of her head, and tell her I love her. She is now oblivious that I am even there. She is rocking and praying eyes closed. I have to leave. I cannot take another moment of watching her do this to her-self again. I ask the nurse to please keep an eye on her, and let them know I will call in when I get home to check on her. I also instruct them to call me if anything happens. I am broken… I sit in my car and cry my eyes out, then I pull myself together, and go home to my family showing a brave front as always.

This is the ugly. The countless times this woman has to go through this. This is her endless adventure in the wonderland of the sick. Her mind, her ugly ugly sick mind, that takes over her beautiful soul, and sucks her up over and over again, and then spitting her out into the darkness. This sick mind that has taken my mother away from me, and has replaced her with this horrific zombie like out of a horror movie, and I am battling it on a daily basis to survive. Its like in all horror movies, the main character survives, and all the others are taken out one by one. So who is the main character her or me?

BI-POLAR

When you think bi-polar so many thoughts run
Through your head...

Yes thoughts running wild out of control,
Isn't that what bi-polar is all about?
Running wild, running crazy,
Cannot seem to stop?

Racing, racing as fast you can, no stopping
Me I am that crazy fan...

Moments forever changing, minute by
Minute, never knowing what is next...

Who will get in my way?
Who can I X-out today?

Sitting here looking around psychotic images
So profound...

Are they going to hurt me?
Who hears my cries?
Do I live or do I die?

Watching dancing lights flashing so bright,
With warped voices shouting in my ear,
Lets get crazy tonight!!!!

Out and about I do go, out of control, does
Anybody know? Can they tell! Are my eyes
Speaking words I cannot say, or am I ignored
Every step of the way...

Then it happens I break free, lost all control
Now everybody can see... Mouth moving,
Unreasonable words come out... I am lost, out
Of my mind, I scream and shout...

I want to hurt you! I want to hurt me!

Can anybody help me, does anybody see?
See me, See me

The real me, not this twisted person who explodes
From time to time,
my sick invisible playmate
Who wants to out shine...

Take a pill; it will be ok, wrapped up in
My bi-polar mind that has gone astray...
Thoughts going crazy inside my head; Do
I live or should I just be dead...

Finish it off be done with it now, bury me six feet
Under ground. Is this the only way to stop
The pain, get rid of my guilt stop all of my
Shame...

Feeling shamed for my illness I cannot control,
And for all that could never understand my
Untraditional wall... This wall of shame, who
Is to blame, my family, my friends, or the
Chemicals in my brain...

Please see me the person I really am,
Filled with love and compassion, who really
Does understand?

CHAPTER 14

My Dad The Lone Eagle Making Peace

Chapter 14

My Dad the Lone Eagle Making Peace

Where to begin? There is so much too say…

My father, he is big and strong, and a force to be reckoned with. This LOUD Italian man with his fu manchu mustache is larger than life. He is a leader, always in control at work and play. He has great conviction, and always feels he is right at all costs. He can be quite self-centered as he feels the world revolves around him. He is a warrior ready to do battle for the ones he loves. He is fearless!

Under all that hardness and bravery is a soft sensitive heart yearning for happiness, and longing for peace. He will never show weakness, but in his dreams he sobs away all his shortcomings and heart breaks. He never sleeps restful, if he actually sleeps at all. He tosses and turns all night long, mumbling the words he cannot say when he is awake. He has too many inner struggles as he silently accepts his pain. This internal anger that eats away at him over the years wearing down his weakened soul.

This man so filled with love of family, and hatred of all who have wronged him.

He would never express his deepest feelings of a family lost, and a heart destroyed.

He would never tell the tale of a mother's indiscretions or a sister's greed, or his disappointment of how he grew up with a mother whom he hated. Only the love of his father, his admiration for an incredible man would flow from his lips.

My father had the type of upbringing that from the outside looking in was the perfect family. Two children spoiled rotten, with hard working parents in the 40s and 50s, when times in the world were changing. A time of all-American baseball and apple pie, God Bless the USA, and Rock Around the Clock.

The reality, my father was an angry young man, just starting his teenage years. His household was dysfunctional and he never really explained the details. I do know his mother cheated on his father, which devastated him, but my inner gut tells me other things went on as well. My dad shared a room with his father, and his sister shared a room with his mother, in the same bed. Does this sound eerily familiar? Amazing how history repeated itself with my mother and I!

As a teen he met my mother and they fell in love, they were 13 yrs old. They had a turbulent relationship from the start. He was an angry teen, and she was a girl who had high anxiety, and depression. They learned how to smoke cigarettes together and to fight together. They broke up several times, but always got back together. They lacked all communications skills necessary to have a healthy relationship, but they truly loved each other and decided to marry in light of all their shortcomings.

Finally out on his own with his beautiful wife in tow, a new home, a great job, he was on top of the world. He worked extremely hard managing a grocery store. As always, he was in charge of the scene. He had strong work ethics, and a strong sense of family. My mother worked hard too, she put herself through hairdressing school and was a top beautician at a high-end salon. They had a great start.

Then along came my brother, and me two years later. The perfect family unit, all of his dreams, has come true. Then like a thief in the night it was all ripped out from underneath him.

His beautiful wife whose mental illness had reared its ugly head, and a child who was dying of Leukemia was now his new world. His only son was taken from him on a spring morning when new life is supposed to be blooming after a long cold winter.

He treasured his children and his little family. He cherished each one of us, and vowed to protect us always. His life is now plummeting out of control, and he is in a total tailspin. He is now dealing with two losses at once. His wife and son, both lost on that spring morning. After Jon Jon's death, my mother was never the same. The small part of her that would shine through from time to time now was gone forever.

This strong man was internally destroyed. He threw himself into his work, the only part of his life that he could control. I always knew he loved me, but as time went on I was now losing my father as well. The father who would take the time to run around the yard with my brother and me, the father that played ball, took us fishing, ice-skating, and swimming was gone. He is now replaced with a hardened shell of a dad broken, totally distraught, holding on by the skin of his teeth, drowning in his pain and anger. As all of these repressed emotions churned inside of him, he became darker by the day.

He now starts drinking heavily and cheating on my mom. He is looking for any type of happiness, but nothing satisfies his thirst. I am now a cloudy image for him, as I remind him of all that he has lost. I am the last piece of a perfect family gone forever.

He is desperate for happiness, searching far and long. When he finally meets someone that eases his pain, and gives him the love he needs to fill that void and help him heal, he runs like a deer! Who could really blame him? His life was unbearable. All that meant anything to him was lost, but in the midst of his cloudy thoughts he forgot something, something very special. He forgot ME!

I resented him greatly for leaving me behind. I resented him for leaving me with the burden and responsibility of my mother. This is something that a young child should never have been left with. I was left alone to be abused. Tortured by the hands of a mother lost in her own turmoil of her sick mind. Tortured by Jerry, a sick twisted individual who saw opportunity and took it. I would think how could he do this to me? I felt worthless for years. Invisible to all because I was continually left behind by everyone!

My father embarked on his new life. With his new wife, and a new daughter, I felt totally left out. I tried so hard to fit the mold of his new family, but this puzzle piece never quite fit.

As my father began to heal, he let me back into his world little by little. We began to get close again, forming a new bond as father and daughter. I felt at times I was a painful reminder of his past, and that is why he kept his distance from me. We were connected not only by father and daughter, but also by tragedy and circumstance. This combination formed an incredible bond, which was something special and treasured. We understood each other beyond words.

He had spent many years hurting, and me resentful. Our powerful love for one another definitely saw us through such a horrible set of circumstances beyond our control.

I did forgive my father for leaving me behind, because even though it was the wrong decision for him to make, I believe he needed to save himself before he could save me. I also believe he did not mean to hurt me. I was an innocent child caught up in this mess. He could not take it anymore and he left.

Could he have really foreseen the future of what would happen to me, when his world was crumbling around his feet? I do not believe if he was in the right state of mind he would of really left me behind.

This is why I forgave him. I could see past all the hurt and pain and felt compassion for him. This was an understanding that we had between the both of us. I do not believe anyone else could really understand it because they were not there from the beginning, when our little family was intact and happy. We did have a short time when we were happy just the four of us. Then when it was gone, it was too much handle. Our deep understanding and love for one another comes for all the joy, pain and heartache we both endured on such different levels. This is the UNSPOKEN TRUTH, binding our souls together forever.

My dad and I became extremely close over the years, and I was a dedicated and loving daughter to him. I would run to his side at a moment's notice during his long illness showing my love and support always. Our close relationship gave me a special gift. It gave him and I a chance to have a conversation before he passed away. This was the hardest conversation that I have ever had to deal with. We talked about our life together, and his coming death. We spoke of family and love, and how we felt we had it all as father and daughter. We had a true understanding of one another and our deep love.

When I flew to his side the last time, our eyes connected and we said it all never muttering one single word. I was blessed to be by his side at the moment he passed. He had all his girls with him, as he wanted. He had my stepmother, my two sisters, and me sitting with him. We all surrounded him, talking to him, playing music, and creating a loving and peaceful environment for this man who suffered for so long. This was our final gift to him, for being the vigilant solider for so many years, dedicating himself to his family in good times and bad. This was our gift to him for making up for lost time, and for overcoming tragedy, and for teaching us strength, courage, fearlessness, and the power of faith.

At the moment of his passing, "Candle in the Wind" plays on the radio, and my brother comes to greet him. He turns his head looks to the corner of the room, and we know Jon-Jon is there. I envision that he takes my fathers hand and guides him home. NO more pain, no more sorrow. We all just put our hands on him and cry. "Lean on Me" is the next song to come across the radio, and we know this is his sign to us to take care of each other, and he will only be a breath away. Lastly, "We are Family," I got all my sisters and me was humming over the radio as we cried together at the realization that he was truly gone.

This vision that I saw the day my father left has come to me in form of dreams. Over and over again, it is always the same. My father and my brother both look back at me and smile. I know they are happy and in peace. This gives me great comfort and another gift from my special family.

Now I talk to him everyday in my mind, and pray for his soul to continue to have peace, never again feeling any pain or sorrow.

Hand in hand with my brother is what I see, both of them smiling down upon us, "Our Guardian Angels."

LEAN ON ME...

On that day of my father's passing my stepmother and sisters and I vowed to take care of each other in my father's honor, as he asked of us. We made a pact that day to move forward with family UNITY. What he taught us over the years about family, loyalty, and pride is the legacy that he wanted us to carry on. His great love of family was endless, and he truly had a heart of gold. On the outside he was tough as nails, but on the inside his soul shined bright!

As time passed there were a lot of changes in the family, some good and some bad. What did not change was my commitment to my stepmother and my sisters. My dad taught me to be loyal always. He always said "family first." I held up my end of the bargin, but three years after his passing my so-called "family" decided to cut me out of their lives for good. I believe jealously and lack of understanding was the motive in regards to one of my sisters, who always seemed to have a chip on her shoulder in regards to me. There were two separate times in our relationship where we cut ties due to her anger and lies. My dad always found a way to pull us back together, but now he is gone and she has this insatiable need to make me her target once again.

When she finally had the opportunity to push me out for good she did, and I learned the true meaning of the phrase "blood is thicker than water," in regards to my stepmother and other sister following in her footsteps, never even trying to understand the reality of what was really going on. I was devastated. The negativity that she projected on to me was just too much to bear, and I gave up trying. It was a battle I was not willing to fight anymore. She brought me to a place where I just didn't want to be. My response was negative and heavy and completely unkind. She struck upon a nerve that could never have a positive outcome. I realized in that moment that our relationship was through. She brought out a side of me that I truly did not like. That is not who I am, and I will never be pushed to that extreme again. It is over.

The hurt that I felt by their rejection was overwhelming. It didn't take them long to replace me with a family friend, like I never existed. That hurt even worse! Imagine being replaced in the blink of an eye, like you never even mattered in the first place? Truly devastating! This is not the family loyalty that my dad taught us! I feel like I do not even know these people anymore, my family is now a bunch of strangers. Did I ever really know them in the first place? Did they really even love me, or was it my dad's love that actually connected us?

I have known my stepmother since I was 11 years old, and the past history that we had together ran extremely deep. For her (especially her) to toss me aside actually blind-sided me in the moment, but now I feel she wanted me out of her life, because I was the last link to my father and the past. By removing me, then all ties to the past are cut for good. Maybe by removing me, she thought the pain would go with it. So our story ends here…

So again, I am left behind, but this time it is different. What my own past has taught me is that no matter how hard it is, you pick yourself up, dust yourself off and move forward. Another quote directly from my father: "Always move forward," and that is exactly what I did!

I know I am blessed with an incredible family and a wonderful circle of friends. My life is rich beyond any amount of money someone could offer me. The lessons I have learned along the way have given me the strength and wisdom to move forward in a positive light.

All of the family values that I was taught by my father live on through me, as I am now teaching my own family. His legacy will always live on, as I am a great example of all the goodness that my father had to offer. Love, loyalty, and pride, those are the three words that describe his family values.

I have moved forward with my life without the girls in it, and I have accepted the fact that they do not want me around anymore. I am not going to say it still doesn't hurt, but these are circumstances beyond my control, and maybe that is where our journey is supposed to end?

I truly believe that people come in and out of our lives for a reason. We may not always know why things happen, but it is all about lessons learned.

It is now almost two years since we have spoken, and they still come to my mind from time to time, and even though we do not speak I wish them well, and I will always love them.

I FORGIVE them for what they have done to me. I forgive them not for them, but for me. By letting go of the anger and resentment I have PEACE in MY heart, and that is a gift I have given to myself.

INTERESTING MOMENT....

After writing this section into the book, I had the opportunity to go see a psychic. I never expected the message that came to me on that day. My father came through, and he spoke about the separation between my family and I, and how even though they treated me poorly to please give it one more shot, and extend myself out to them, and if nothing happens then you know you tried your best. I was floored. My dad did send me many wonderful messages that day, from telling me how much he loved me, and apologizing for being so hard on me. He apologized for how much pain I had to endure while growing up. It was so moving and powerful, that words cannot truly describe it. "HEALING."

I am not asking you to believe in psychics, as we all have our own beliefs, but that day changed me in many ways. I felt such love from my dad, and such release of so many feelings, it was like a new awakening for me.

With much hesitation, I did reach out to my stepmother and explained to her what had happened. I did tell her that I did not have any intension of reaching out, but I was listening to the words of my dad. Honestly, I did not know how she was going to respond, as it has been so long since we have spoken. I was pleasantly surprised by her kindness and openness to all of this. We are now speaking once again, and trying to re-establish a relationship. It will never be the same as it was before, and I have not heard from either one of my sisters, but it is a start. So this is another chapter in my life that has a "to be continued" attached to it.

Again, I was pleasantly surprised to hear from both of my sisters. One stepped forward, and we were able to clear up our differences, and move forward. We both decided to let it all rest and focus on the future with understanding and kindness.

My youngest sister came last, and we have re-established our relationship as well. I am happy that we have all moved forward and reconnected, it was the right thing to do. Bottom line we truly love each other. Maybe we needed the seperation to heal and understand what truly is important in life, and that is family.

So I guess the lesson here is never say never!!

☙ MAKING PEACE ❧

*A man – Strong and sweet - A man proud no defeat
Standing tall that is he, never weak no liability…*

My earliest memory of he is of laughter, of pain, so strong, sometimes mean… Always hiding his defects so nobody could see…

*Drowned in his work, long hours he seeks, running
From memories he keeps so deep… The pain for him,
It breaks through like a river, rapids out of control cutting the brow of his forehead with crevices so deep, they are like gapping holes, a river running out of control… He hides, he runs, trying to save his soul…*

*Years have past, his battle scars all collected… His
Pain hidden by day, but not in his sleep – restless is he, when he closes his eyes, no peace at bedtime; it all comes out — back to life…*

Every waking memory all the hurt and pain, travels through his mind making him privately insane… The silent torture he lives inside of his brain… Who could ever know the depth of his pain?

*He is strong and confident, no time to be weak, but he is
A sad little child every night in his sleep… He mumbles, he weeps, and cries out in pain, the rage, the anger who is to blame; the one's who truly love him, really understand his game…*

All we can do is hope and pray, that his pain will pass some how, some day... This MAN I see right before my own eyes... My Father, My Rock, A Very Special Guy...

Dedicated to my Dad who has left this earth on April 27, 2010... I love you, Daddy, ALWAYS AND FOREVER

FROM OUT OF THE DARKNESS, NEW BEGININGS ...

THE DARK PLACE

The realm of hell this deep dark place inside my soul...

Hurt buried so deep, where I eternally weep...

Thoughts roll through my mind, tales as old as TIME...
Oh this place, there is no sleep, just constant Emotional heap...

Rolling hills, a natural disaster, where there is NO happily ever after...
Words twisted horrendous pain, mind warped full of shame...

How did I get here, broken emotionally, full of fear...
Fighting so hard to keep it tight, battling against the evil strife...

My personal hell inside my mind, this dark place, NO sunshine...
Alone I weep stability creeks, a flood of tears - Pure Heartbreak, too Many years!
Racing moving at the speed of light, this emotional train wreck, the story of My life!

Moving so quick, no slowing down, not even time to look around...

Full speed ahead is the words I hear, this hypnotic conductor whispering
In my ear - NO STOPPING from here on out, no time to scream and shout...

How am I to keep up the pace, out of control NO personal space...

Someone pull the emergency brake please bring me to a halt down
On my knees... Praying for a time to slow down, finally get a chance to touch ground...

Getting in control of my life, this personal goal, winning the good fight
Learning to let go is all I hear, your personal teacher is right here...

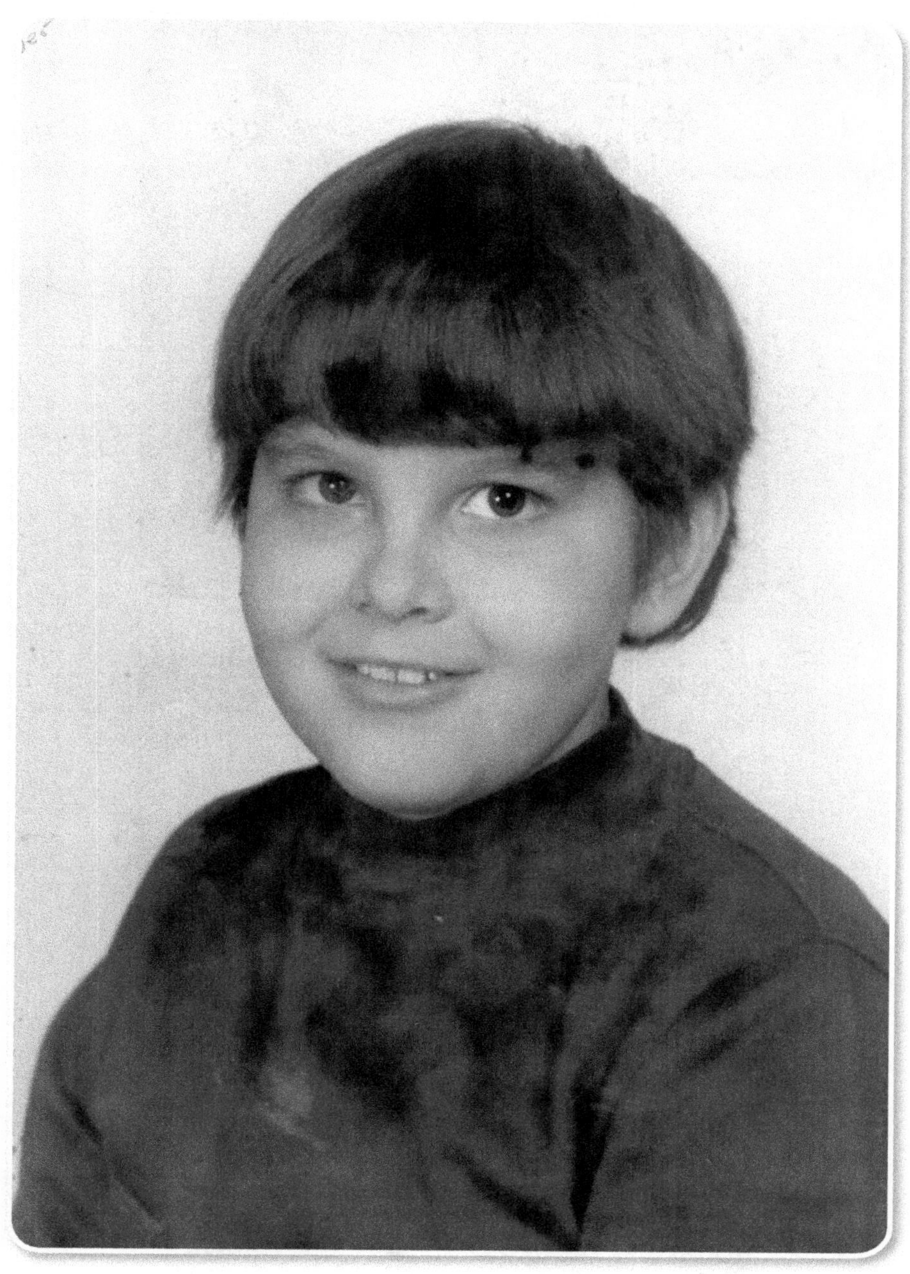

I Love you ♡ I Love you

To Lisa
from John
I Love you
♡ I Love
Lisa

CHAPTER 15

Seas of The Unknown

Chapter 15

Seas of the Unknown

A New Chapter in My Life:

High school is now behind me. I feel like I left the past on the steps of my high school on the day I graduated. It feels good, like some of the past pain has been released, and I can focus on my future, with better things to come. I am preparing to go to college, and I cannot wait for it to start. I engross myself in my work as I wait for my starting date.

One rainy day I run out to pick up my paycheck, as I wanted to do some shopping to get new clothing for school when it happened. I got into an automobile accident. It all happened so fast, and just like that my car was totaled.

. I couldn't believe this was happening. I lost control on wet roads and went into a full spin. I was going up a hill when it happened. A woman was coming down the hill, and tried to pass me while I was spinning out of control. Just as she reached me my car came out of the spin and I shot like a bullet across the road and hit her. I wrecked my knee, and hit my head, but I was ok. The other woman was shaken, but ok as well. I am feeling like this is another roadblock for me to move forward, and I am hysterical. How am I going to get to school? How am I going to get to work? My dad cannot get another car for me, and my mother is useless. I cannot depend on my boyfriend because he needs his car to go to school and work. I just lost my freedom. I cannot be stuck back in that house with no way out. I will go crazy. As the police officer calls my dad and explains the situation, he tells the cop to have the car towed, and he will speak with me later. My dad did not want to talk to me, at that moment he was furious.

Of course my mother was like, it's a sign from God that you need to stay home with me. I need you! I think you should quit school. I am like, What! Quit school before I start? No way.

Here is our conversation on that day.

The police officer gives me a ride home. I hobble in the door, and my mother starts screaming. What is wrong with you, what is wrong with you? I say, "Mom I got into a car accident and totaled my vehicle." Oh My God, she says. "It's the devil coming after me, he is trying to get to me through you. Oh my God what are we going to do? Motherfuckers!!" She is screaming this pumping her fist up to the sky. My grandparents enter the room, and ask what happened. I explain the whole story, and my mother is now rocking in her chair, ready to blow again. "Lisa, you know what this means right?" I say, "No, what?" "This means that you are not meant to go to school, and you have to stay home with me." I was like, No way Mom, I am not staying home with you. "Lisa, you need to, God is telling you." No he is not, Mom. "Yes, he is, you are meant to take care of me, I need you, you cannot leave me ever." My grandmother interrupts her. "Joann, she is going to school now stop that." She turns to me and simply says, "Lisa, you can take the city bus, just find out the bus routes and times." I look at her appalled. She cannot see, but she can feel my disgust, and says, "Lisa, it is either that or nothing, and take that sour look off your face!" "Ok, Grandma I will find out, and I will take the bus." My grandmother was such a sensible woman, always finding a solution to a problem without even raising her voice. Also, it was amazing how she knew how I would react without even seeing me; she blew me away all the time!

"Grandpa can drive you to work, and maybe even Mark can pick you up sometimes or even your father."

My mother chimes in. "That selfish mother-fucker won't take time out from his whore bag family to help my Lisa!" She spits on the floor mumbling and glaring, lighting up a cigarette.

My grandfather finally speaks up and says, "Joann knock it off, we will all help her, she needs to go to school and work, so shut up!"

"Go Fuck yourself, Dad, and the horse you road in on." She then gets up and storms off to the bedroom. She lies on the bed, and starts crying and mumbling, she is smoking, crying, laughing all by her self. You could her obscene words coming from down the hall. We all ignore her.

I finally talk to my dad, and he is angry and yells at me. I cried like a baby, and tried to explain. With my dad, there was no explaining—he yells and you take it. So, that is what I did. I did get sympathy from my boyfriend Mark, who said he would help when he could.

Summer was here, and Mark was working at a grocery store, and I started school. Every morning I would make my way down the hill to the bus stop at 6:30 a.m. I head off to school. On the way home I would start my homework on the bus. I would make my way up the hill come in the house have a snack, do more homework, and get ready for work. I would come home from work, finish my homework, shower, and go to bed. Sometimes I would not go to bed until 1 a.m. I worked six days a week, plus school full time. I did this every day, and made sure all my schoolwork was done no matter how late I was up. If I didn't have a ride to work, I would walk. When my mom was capable of driving she would drive me. I would get rides from anyone who would help me out. I was going to make this work, no matter what it took. It was so hard to juggle everything but I was determined to succeed. I even sucked it up with my mother to get rides. It killed me, but I held my tongue. Her new thing was, now that I got into an accident, I wasn't capable of driving her car, so I was not allowed to. I laughed at that because I had been driving her crazy ass around since I was 12, and now I am not capable. This was another way to control me, but I wasn't going to let her. I found other ways to get to work. I only used her when I absolutely had to.

It was hard for me to lose that freedom. I had a lot of anxiety over it, because it was hitting a nerve with me, inside where everything was buried. I could feel that past pain of being trapped, and feeling like there is no escape. It pounded in my head every moment that I actually had time to think. I always did the same thing, push it away and bury it. I started burying things so deep, that I could not even verbally communicate those feelings. I would just get angry, and then I would lash out and say the most horrible things. I learned this behavior from my mother for sure. The wicked things that I would say, especially to her, were horrible. Sometimes, it would come out onto others if they crossed my path the wrong way. I was quick to respond, as I was always afraid of loosing the upper hand. I needed to have control, and be in control at all costs. This is how I trained myself to survive.

My own coping skills that helped me over come my horrible past, is now coming back to haunt me, even holding me back on certain aspects in my life. I struggled a lot. Every day I would have to remind myself to hold my tongue, and stay in control. I would mentally talk to myself all the time, so I would remain focused on what was important. I would even write things down, and re-read them over and over again. My journal was full of thoughts and quotes, helping me to stay in control of my emotions. It was extremely hard, but the bigger picture, my future, is what I held on to. My hopes and dreams carried me along.

I do have to say I did get educated on the city bus. I took the bus from West Haven to New Haven. My school was on the corner of Church and Chapel St. This was near the green and Yale University. I had to travel through the worst sections of town before my stop. I saw everything from homeless people to prostitutes. I remember one day sitting on the bus going home, when this woman gets on in a dark blue ball gown. Of course she sits right next to me. I am doing my homework, and try not to make eye contact. Well it didn't matter because she had things to say.

Hey, hey you look at me, she says. I look up from my book, annoyed. "Can I help you?" I respond. She is rocking feverishly and sweating like a pig, and who could blame her it was summer in the city, 95 degrees, and she is in a ball gown. This was so classic for New Haven! You are a pretty girl, I love your long hair, and sexy eyes, you should come work for me, and she is now licking her lips at me, grunting.

I am totally grossed out, and say, "Can you just leave me alone." She gets pissed and quips, "Hey white bitch I am offering you a job as a high end prostitute, and you givin' me attitude, I should slice you up!"

"Look I just want to be left alone, I do not need your fucking job you stupid black crazy bitch now leave me the hell alone!" She jumps up, I am thinking for sure she is going to attack me, and of course everyone on the bus is ignoring the situation. Then, all of a sudden she starts screaming on the top of her lungs, "I got to get out of here, I got to get out of here, they are coming for me!" The bus driver pulls over opens the door, and she bolts out the door, running down the street screaming. He closes the door pulls away and it was like it never happened. People never want to get involved, and I learned quickly to stand up for myself. That was the first of many strange encounters on the bus. Every morning it was the smelly old man who would sit next to me. Every afternoon it was a crazy person, or a woman with five kids screaming and slapping them around, or the drunk who proceeded to throw up on himself. It was never dull, and I always tried to sit next to someone that looked halfway normal and just engross myself in my schoolwork.

Every morning I would make the pilgrimage down the hill to the bus, then deal with the ride, handle school and the stresses that went along with it, and back on the bus for the crazy ride home. Day in and day out through all kinds of weather, I just endured it. I was on a mission, and nothing was going to bring me down.

Fall was upon us, and the falling leaves brought great depression to my mom as it does every year. She says when the leaves fall off the trees, it's like all the angels in heaven are dying and my brother was rotting. This particular fall seemed worse then normal for her, if you could image that. Usually it's just the depression, then my birthday would roll around and Christmas, and she would perk up until New Year, and then it was down hill again.

My mom stopped taking her medicine, and was getting increasingly worse. One night I came home from work, and she was sitting at the famous kitchen table where all the action seemed to happen, our focal point of the household. It was rare to come into the house and not find someone sitting there. It didn't matter what time of day or night somebody was always up at my house, even the dog.

I walk in the door, and she is glaring, face all twisted. I just say, "Hey Mom," trying to keep it light. "I know you were out whoring around tonight, having sex with all those men!" Mom, please not tonight I am exhausted, and have homework to do. Homework, what homework sucking that big dick! I know you were doing it Lisa, I saw it with my own eyes. You were with all those men tonight. "Mom, you need to get a grip, and stop you, were dreaming or what ever you do when you are not taking your medicine." Well that was it, she came lunging at me grabbing me by the throat, and started choking me screaming slut, whore, cunt any nasty word that would come out of her mouth. I try to get her off me, but she has such adrenaline that she over powers me. I cannot breathe, I am gasping, and now she is hitting my head on the door. My grandfather comes running, and my grandmother makes her way down the hall. He is screaming at her to stop, and grabs her. She pushes him, and he falls back.

I manage to escape, and I run around the kitchen table. My poor grandmother is screaming, "Joann stop, stop it right now!" My grandfather is now yelling as well. My mother threatens to kill me, so I grab her keys and flee from the house. She runs after me, but my grandfather stops her from coming out the door. I am hysterical, but I jump in the car and speed away as fast as I can. I just drive, and I keep on driving for a long time. I didn't know where to go. I didn't want to bother my dad because of the baby and it was late. I didn't want to bother my boyfriend either, but I knew he would have been calling me and if I didn't answer he would have been worried, so I drove to his house. It was about midnight. I knock on the door, and his father answers. I am crying, and he tells me to come in and gets Mark. His father was such a kind man, and looked so sympathetic when asking me if I was ok. I just shook my head, and sat down.

Mark and I sat outside on the steps for a long time. I told him what happened, and cried a lot. He just listened, and asked me what I was going to do. I said I would give her time to cool off, and then I would go back home. I had school in the morning, and could not miss a day. I was so distraught. I am tired. I am stressed and just sickened by her nasty behavior. I honestly do not know what will happen next. Mark doesn't say too much about it, because he knows I have to go back and I will. He hates what is going on, but knows right now I have no choice so he just supports me.

I finally make it home about 2 a.m. My grandfather is waiting up for me. I come in the door, and he says, "You ok?" I say yes. Your mom went to bed so you should be fine. Ok, I am going to take a shower, and do my homework. My grandfather makes coffee for me, and sits with me while I do my homework. He doesn't say much, but I can tell the whole thing shook him up. About an hour later my grandmother comes out. "Lisa, are you here?" she says as she enters the kitchen. "Yes, Grandma, I am doing my homework. Grandpa made me coffee, do you want me to get you a cup?" That would be great she said. She sits down sipping her coffee quietly and then says, "What are we going to do with your mother?" My grandfather says, "Can we sell her!" and starts laughing. We all chuckling for a moment, as he was trying to lighten the mood. Then we all get serious, and I say, "Grandma we have to call the doctor, she needs to go to the hospital before she hurts someone, or herself." I know Lisa, I know. I will call your aunt in the morning, and have her call. I hope she goes without a fight. I cannot stand hearing all that fuss. Grandma you know better than that, she will go out kicking and screaming. I just hope it happens before I come home from school tomorrow. My Grandmother responds, "I don't know Lisa, I don't understand. Why she is so weak?" Grandma, she is sick. Then there was silence. A silence I was all too familiar with. A silence that broke my heart, leaving me internally damaged forever.

Well, my mom went back to the hospital putting up a horrible fight. She went out in hand cuffs, screaming and spitting the whole way. I was so happy she was gone. I needed a break from her. We all needed a break from her. She created so much chaos in the house. She was quite angry when I spoke with her on the phone, and told me I better talk to her every day or she would break out and hunt me down. I told her I would try to talk to her as much as possible. I reminded her about school and work. She responded with to hell with all that shit I am your mother, and that is all that matters, GET IT!! Yes, I get it.

I went on with my life, enjoyed having a room to myself for the first time in a very long time, and I loved every minute of it. I still took the bus to school, but at times I would drive my mom's car to work. I had a little bit of freedom, and room to breathe. I felt new and refreshed. My mood lightened and I felt some happiness. Of course that happiness was crushed every time I spoke with her on the phone or visited her. She knew which buttons to push to bring me down in about 2 seconds. She was a professional, cutting anyone down in a heartbeat with her venomous words. She could make anyone cry, even my father who was tough as nails. I witnessed it countless times in the past.

She was gone for two months, and then just before Christmas she was home. The party was over. My little vacation from her was done. She was back with a vengeance. She was still off, and we all had to walk on eggshells for a while, until she settled back down. She was like a tornado, totally unpredictable, and it was always awkward and strange at our house. It's hard to live this way…

The holiday came and went, school was progressing, and I was now taking the bus through the winter, dealing with the snow, sleet and freezing weather every day. I asked my dad to buy me a heavy winter coat for Christmas, long and waterproof, and he did. I armed myself with all that I needed to survive out there. I knew how to take care of myself, and I was not going to let winter slow me down. I kept pushing forward.

Mark and I were having some bumps in our relationship now. He was still in high school, and I was in college. We both worked, so there was not a lot of time for us to see each other. He was a great guy, but he was always jealous, so we would fight. The less time we spent together the worse it would get. Before I knew it winter was over, and spring was here. Mark and I were holding it together, and his senior prom was fast approaching. He was going to be graduating high school, and I was going to be graduating college. It was an exciting time. I was still babysitting my sister on the weekends, and enjoying our time. I was getting along with my dad and his wife for the most part, which was good. My mom finally settled down for a while after my brother's birthday and anniversary of his death. Things were moving along, and I was looking forward to getting out of school. I would daydream of finding an awesome job, and moving out on my own.

When June arrived we both graduated. We were happy that it was over for the both of us, and we could try and move forward with our relationship. We really were committed to making it work. We started to get along better, but there were still issues with his mom being controlling. I tried to ignore it, and just concentrated on us, but she made it hard. He would always defend her, so I didn't even bother to argue about it anymore, as I felt I would just do my own thing anyway. I understood his loyalty to his mother, but the thought of her controlling him or me for that matter, made me crazy.

Summer of 1984 had arrived, and once again life was changing. I found a job at a Medical Surgical Center in New Haven as a secretary. I really threw myself into my work, and made sure I did everything right. I was feeling really good about myself, and thought about the money I would make so I could get a new car. Until then I was still taking the bus. One day I was waiting at the bus stop eager to get home after a long day at work, when these girls started fighting next to me. One pulled out a switchblade and sliced the other girl's face wide open from her eye to her chin. Blood flew everywhere, even on me. She was screaming, and the other girls went running. I was shocked at such an act of violence right there, but I tried to help her until the ambulance came. I kept on reassuring her it would be ok. Of course I missed my bus, and by the time I got home it was really late. I was sitting on the bus with blood all down my shirt, and not one person asked me if I was ok. The bus harbored a strange set of people oblivious to all that was around them. They were like zombies just riding, waiting for the bell to ring to cue them to get off. At that moment, I decided it was time to buy a car, some how, some way.

THE NEXT STEP...

With the help of my uncle and my father, I bought a used car. I took out a small loan to pay for it. I am 19 yrs old, fresh out of college, with a full time job, a car loan, a student loan, my own phone bill and insurance. I felt so grown up. I worked hard. I felt accomplished. I learned how to manage my money well, and I also learned how to save. I was feeling happy, but that was short lived!

I had to stay late at work one evening to get some extra things done. I was sitting at my desk when the boss comes in. He was a tall man with curly hair of Jewish descent. He was a little beefy. At first he was making small talk with me, and I did not think anything of it. Then it all changed. He came over and put his hands on my shoulders, and started rubbing me telling me how beautiful I was. He then went on to say if I wanted to move forward in the company I needed to work up to his expectations. I was shocked. I was freaked out, and sat frozen for a moment. I was getting flash backs of Jerry taking control of me in such a way. I then snapped back into reality, and jumped up out of my seat. I told him to stop, and I was working just fine. He said that he needed more from me, and if I was not willing to give more then I may not have a future there. He went on to say we should go out for drinks after work. I said to him you realize I am only 19. He said, I know and I love that. I was totally grossed out, and packed up my stuff and left. He said to me as I was walking out the door to think about it. I just kept on walking.

It was Friday so I had all weekend to stew over it in silence. I decided I would go back to work on Monday and pretend that it never happened. I figured if I just worked then he would leave me alone. I was so naive.

Work became awkward after that night, and I made the mistake of telling one of the other secretaries about what happened. She told me he made advances on her as well, but what I didn't know was that she was having an affair with him, and he was married. He stopped talking to me, and the following week he called me into his office and let me go. He said I was not working out, and he wished me luck on my future successes. I was so angry, and I told him exactly what I thought of him. He did not care one bit, and just handed me my pink slip, and told me to leave or he would have me escorted out. I looked down at my pink slip, and under the part where it states reason for being let go was this…

Did not work out because was unable to take detailed phone messages.

That was it! As I walked out, I looked back at him and said, "You're a fat piece of shit!" To which he screamed at me "GET OUT." Chills ran through my body, as I felt defeated. He took advantage of me, and I could do nothing but walk away. Once again I was feeling broken down. I was feeling worthless as I made my way to my car. I cried the whole way home. I felt like a failure. Then I started to think about all my bills. I just got this car, now was it going to be taken away from me like everything else in my life? I was in a full blown panic attack by the time I reached my driveway.

I ran in the house, and my grandmother was at the table. I sat down and cried, and told her everything. She was so angry. She said if she could see, she would drive down there and beat him up! She said I should write a letter to the president of the company, and explain what had happened to me. So that is what I did. I wrote an extremely mature letter stating what happened to me, and how this made my first professional work experience a joke. I mailed it out, and started looking for a job right away.

My dad wanted me to work for the City of West Haven. He knew somebody who could get me in immediately. I told him I didn't want to do that. I wanted to work at Mile's Pharmaceuticals with my cousin. She told me there was an opening in her department, and she would put in a good word for me. I really wanted this job, and I was determined to get it. My father was so pissed at me because I refused the job he found for me, but I saw bigger things for myself. I did not want to be that defeated little girl anymore. After what had happened to me on my first job, I was even more motivated to find something bigger and better. I was once again going to prove I was worth it.

At the moment I was fired, I felt so small and defeated, but it didn't last too long because I was fueled by determination to succeed. I stood up to the boss by writing the letter. I stood up to my father by telling him that I didn't want to work at the town hall, and I went into the interview for the job at Mile's with confidence. I sat with the boss, and told him the truth about what happened and why I was really fired. I even explained to him how it affected me, as this was my first professional position. I also told him that I wanted to work for him because I saw what it did for my cousin. I went on to say I was inspired by how much she had learned from being there, and how much she respected him. I wanted the opportunity to better myself, and learn new things. He smiled at me, and his kind blue eyes said it all. I felt great about my interview, and prayed I would get this job. When I walked out of that office, I held my head up high and no matter what the outcome was going to be, I knew I did my best.

Two days later he offered me the job. He told me he respected my honesty and maturity at such a young age. He loved my confidence, and expected great things out of me. I was now part of a medical research team. I worked for a group of six doctors and four other secretaries. Once again I felt on top of world. My father told me he was proud of me for going after what I wanted. It felt good to hear those words come out of his mouth. I could not wait to start on this new venture. I received a letter from the president of the Medical Surgical Center stating their apologizes for what had happened, and wished me luck in the future. That was it. I am not sure if they believed me or not, but at least I got a response, and was able to put closure on this horrible experience. I could now move forward.

Mark didn't seem as happy as I thought he would be. I guess it was because he was feeling insecure as I was moving forward on new levels, and he was still working at the grocery store and attending a business college for computers. He was not happy with school, and really did not know what he wanted to do with his future. We were once again growing apart. I was moving forward and he was stuck. It started to weigh on our relationship.

CHANGES... ALWAYS CHANGES...

Here we are back to fall again. My mother is acting up, as it is her cue as the leaves fall. I am starting a new job, and her antics are putting pressure on me. I juggle it the best that I can. I start picking up extra hours at work. I want to impress my boss, and show my commitment to the company. I definitely had my shortcomings. When my mother was acting up, it affected my work. I was sleep deprived, and cranky. I tried to stay focused, but at times it was hard.

When my work started to get sloppy, our head secretary pulled me in the office, and preceded to tell me I could be let go if my work continued to decline. I was quite upset, as this job meant everything to me. I asked her to please give me another chance, and I will not let her down, and she agreed! I worked so hard from that moment forward. I was terrified of failure. I double checked my work, sometimes triple checked my work to make sure I was doing it right. When I walked in the door of my office I had to put everything else out of my head. I needed to keep it separate, and remain focused on the tasks at hand. My mom would call me at work a lot, and I would always remind her that I could get in trouble, but of course she didn't care. She was being the self-centered bitchy person that she always was. I was now juggling two different worlds, and learned to play my parts well. I was totally professional at work, and on the home front I was the caretaker of my mother, and helping with the decision making of her care. I was also the attentive girlfriend, the responsible sister, and the good daughter to my dad. I played every part to the best of my ability. My life was a circus, and I was the star juggler.

My mother took another downward spiral, and by November she was back in the hospital again. She was there about a month or so. She always made it back home in time for Christmas. She was so predictable. I knew she would not miss the holiday, as this was her big celebration, before the great depression of the New Year. She would start in January and it would last through April. She would pine for my brother, curse my father, and torture me. She had rituals that she would do daily, and she would repeat cycles over and over again.

Living with someone who is so ill was extremely difficult. My grandparents had their own health issues, and they were old school. They did not understand her at all. I did understand her, but it did not make it much easier on a daily basis. Sometimes, I would come home on my lunch hour to check in on her. It helped my grandmother when I did, as my mom would lighten up on her. I was committed to her, even though I didn't want to be. I always tried to make everyone happy. I tried to keep balance, but most of the time I was lost in transition. I rarely took any time for myself to do what I wanted to do. When I did get a chance to get out, I would go to the gym, take my dog for a walk on the beach, or paint and draw. I enjoyed swimming at the high school pool, and would go lap swimming when I had a chance. It was a great form of release for me. I always felt better after a good walk or swim. My days were full, and I was still moving forward. I was saving my money, and working 6 days a week.

My hard work started to pay off. My boss noticed how committed I was, and how much my work had improved. I was now responsible for working on the computer change over in our department. We went from Wang's to IBM's (talk about dating myself here), and all the charts, reports and files had to be converted over. This was a huge job, and a lot of responsibility. I worked side by side with my cousin, to complete this task. We spent countless nights and weekends, sometimes even working 7 days straight without a break. When we finally finished the conversion, our boss said we did a phenomenal job, and we were well rewarded for our dedication and hard work. Our boss treated us well, and always gave us incentives to work harder. He even took us on business trips to NYC for medical conferences, as he felt we were the core part of the team. He even gave us spending money on one trip to NYC, and sent us off shopping at Macy's for the afternoon. He was one in a million that's for sure! We went out for group luncheons, and happy hour on Friday's. He always treated. He would call them our business field trips to get us out of the office. So we worked even harder for him, and I was feeling quite grown up. He was inspirational, and always gave us positive feedback on what we were working on, and great pointers to better ourselves along the way. He was like a teacher, so to speak, always using a situation as the next great lesson. We learned a lot from him.

I was now associating with an older crowd, and Mark was not happy. He left school because it was not what he wanted to do. He decided to work full time at the grocery store and took a position on the overnight crew for more money and experience. Our time was becoming even more limited, and his growing jealously was a major issue. My kind and sweet boyfriend was turning into a tyrant. He did not want me out after work, and hanging out with my colleagues. He became suspicious and untrusting, and his kind words have now turned into sarcastic metaphors. When we were together it was painstaking, and I counted the minutes until I was free from under his judgmental thumb! I told him that was too bad if he didn't like me going out, and I was going to do what I needed to do for myself. I was committed to my job and my coworkers. His response was, "You're supposed to be committed to me!"

As spring was coming to a close, and summer was fast approaching, changing of the seasons was inevitable, as my world was ever changing.

SEAS OF THE UNKNOWN

Unseen, untold, this tragic case
Of a beauty – Story unfolds...

Not knowing the case, this sole stands
Before you – your twisted image.
Can you see your fate?

The past buried so deep, lost in the
Depths of the pit inside the mind, clouded
Never to be found, just glimmers,
Sneak peaks, as the tragedy unfolds piece
By piece looking for release...

This island, untouchable in the ocean of
Pain, incredible storm, drowned by rain...

Children chanting, "RAIN RAIN GO AWAY,"
These imaginary voices here to stay - Fighting
Off the images, grandstanding all the way!

Visions of sugar plums dance in your head, one
By one you wish they were dead!
Sugary sweet, sour defeat, lost thoughts the
Destructive kind, obviously loosing your mind...

Lost you are waiting to be found, this sick
Fairytale, bazaar too profound to speak it out
Loud.

Would anyone believe how twisted the
Words too horrible to speak?

Holding it inside your head, ready to explode,
OH how you dread the day it all breaks free, Volcano
Erupts, hits open seas. As the waves hit hard,
Listening to the sounds, haunting so loud...
Echoes of voices carry through
The air...

"True Freedom must come from within,
Let the evil fairytale go take your final swim"

CHAPTER 16
Complicated I Am and Seasons of Beauty

Chapter 16

Complicated I Am And Seasons of Beauty

Summer of 1985 was in full bloom, and I was starting to really live life. I was established in my career, making good money, and starting to enjoy things. I shopped all the time, and bought fantastic clothing for work and play. I felt I deserved to treat myself after all my hard work. I was still very careful with my money, but I did let loose a little. I wanted to look my best all the time, and carried myself with great confidence. Work was going incredible, and I was absorbing every moment of it. I felt I was at my best when I was working. I had a purpose, and I was a part of something special.

On the home front, things were the same. I was still trapped in that same bedroom with my mother, forced to sleep in the same bed, and deal with her daily antics. Family was still coming and going. I now had a great relationship with my grandparents, and looked forward to spending time with them, when I was actually home. We would laugh over coffee in the morning, and chatted late into the evening when I would finally stroll through the door. I was learning to appreciate them for who they were, and what they represented. Now that I was growing up, I had a better understanding of how their life was, and how it played out for them. I respected them, and listened to their stories and advice, which helped me really see the bigger picture. I loved them dearly, and was grateful that we were able to get to this place together. I cherish those moments, and hold them dear to my heart.

I was definitely living in two different worlds at the same time. I would go to work and be this confident young woman who seemed to have the world at my fingertips, and then once I walked into that house on the hill it was back to being trapped in the room with my mother and all the memories that could destroy my outer world. I was the constant juggler, switching hats with each environment that I stepped into. It was hard, but I was very good at it, switching my role to adapt to any situation. That is one thing that my horrible past taught me, was how to adapt to anything, no matter how bad it was. It was a double-edged sword, as it is good to be able to adapt, but at what cost?

My relationship with my dad was on the mend too. We re-established our father/daughter relationship, and had a deeper understanding of one another. We still had our moments of disagreements, but had mutual respect for our opinions. I was happy for him that he was able to reinvent himself, and start a new family. I didn't feel as much of an outsider, as I had in the past. There were still moments, when I would get those pings of old feelings, and sadness, but I decided if I wanted a relationship with him, I had to put it to rest. I have to say for the most part I did, but there were certain things that would never go away, and I just accepted that for what it was. I loved my father dearly, and I knew I wanted him in my world.

Mark and I were having serious issues in our relationship. I was growing at a rapid pace, and it was like he was standing still. We could not agree on anything, and fought all the time. We did decide to take a vacation together, and see where our relationship was. We thought that if we were away from everything, we could reconnect again. Our vacation was a lot of fun, but I felt like we were more like friends enjoying each other's company, then a young couple in love. I realized during that vacation that I loved Mark, but I was not in love with him. I had grown up, and he hadn't. I was very aware of how I handled things now compared to the way he was handing things. We were now total opposites. This trip was bittersweet for me, as I learned even more about myself, and what I wanted for my future.

We came back from that vacation with two different outlooks. He felt it was great for us, and we were more in love than ever. He spoke of marriage and kids. I knew it was over. I didn't know what to do. I thought, "How could we go on the same vacation and see things so differently?" I felt obligated to him, as he was there for me through all my hard times with my mother. He was a vigilant soldier by my side through all my high school dilemmas, always having my back. My father loved him, and so did the family. Everyone loved him but me. I knew I would always love him as a person and respect the dedication that he showed me over our time together, but I also knew I needed that inner passion with someone, and that someone was not him. I out grew him.

I was conflicted as I felt it was my duty to stay with him, as I did not want to hurt him. I loved the fact that he supported me the way he did, and how caring he was. Our relationship taught me how to love, and how to be loved. It taught me how to be intimate with a man, and to feel love and tenderness, not pain and abuse. I learned the difference between a good relationship and a bad one.

Deep in my heart, I knew I'd outgrown him, and I was ready to move on. I wanted that deep, deep love. I wanted to look at my partner, and feel complete and total love. I wanted a soul mate to share my life with, a grown up relationship. I knew it was not with him. I was at a cross road in my life, and it made me sad. I think I was also afraid to let go of our relationship, because that meant truly letting go of that part of my life. The stepping stone that got me to where I was at that exact moment in time. I had grown up. In the middle of all that mess, I grew up. The realization was amazing and scary at the same time. I still had all this baggage, but I was also renewed. I was changed. Mark helped me get there, and I will be forever grateful to him for loving me the way he did. He gave me the strength to keep on moving forward, and it was with that great strength that I had to let him go.

Fall of 1985 was upon us. Summer was over, the vacation was done, and I had a lot to think about. I still have not expressed my true feelings to Mark, and was faking it for the sake of everyone but myself. This is so me, wanting to make everyone else happy, and putting myself last. I was so sad inside. I felt empty. I felt like my mom, the leaves were falling, and I was depressed. The last thing in the world that I wanted was to be like her. It was a horrible feeling. She was depressed, and so was I. I totally threw myself into my work, as this was my comfort zone.

I was working hard, and our building was getting a make over at this time. They added on a new section, and our team would be moving soon. I engrossed myself into what was going on at work. I kept myself extremely busy, and spent little time with Mark, blaming it on work, as not to make him suspicious of how I was feeling. He was a smart man, and knew something was up, but he played along. I feel he did because he was hoping I would come around. He was buying his time, as he did not want to loose me. I know he loved me deeply, and truly wanted to spend the rest of his life with me. This was a heavy burden for me that was weighing heavier and heavier as the days and weeks went on. I was tormented by guilt and loyalty. I would think, "How can I hurt someone who has been so loyal and compassionate to me?" I was totally conflicted in my thoughts.

We started fighting again, and it was unbearable. We fought every time we saw each other. I would go see him at lunchtime a lot because of his work schedule. I tried really hard to be kind and stay connected but, he would always find something to start a fight with me about, and it was mostly stupid things. Mark became extremely petty. It seemed that his internal anger about our relationship or lack of so to speak was getting the best of him. I also felt guilty over that as well. One more thing to throw on the pile of guilt!

His mother was always there to witness the bickering, but surprisingly, she stayed quiet. As I would leave his house she would always give me the evil eye, as to say stop hurting my son! She definitely did not see my point of view at all. I respected that, as she was his mother and did not want to see her son hurt, so I would give her a half smile as I left, and I would go back to work crying. When I pulled in the parking lot I would suck it up, hold my head up high and throw myself back into my job. Once again switching hats effortlessly, but internally I was paying one hell of a price. I was angry that I was feeling this way, and I knew I had to make tough choices. I always heard the term growing pains, but never put much thought into it, but now I knew exactly what they were talking about. I felt totally trapped, and I needed to find a way out. I was suffocating, and my anxiety level was on an all time high. I was preoccupied in my own thoughts, and at the same time trying to stay focused on what needed to be done. What an emotional transformation I was going through. I felt like things were coming at me in all directions. At this point I was just trying to keep my head above water until I could sort it all out. I was doing a lot of soul searching, and putting different scenarios together in my mind to see what made sense.

Lots of confusion…

☙ COMPLICATED I AM ❧

Wanting to be care free, a free spirit full of laughter and cheer, but
Weighed down by the responsibilities bestowed upon me for years... From
The time of my youth, responsibility was my suit, playing out the hand I was
Dealt, not an easy one, so I play it with a bet...

It's been a long and winding road for me, filled with pain, joy and pure misery... This complicated life I have led, most others may have wound up dead... trying to fight off the evil and hate all around, looking for the light, trying to keep my feet on the ground...

Happiness is what I wanted to see, putting away all my hurt and misery, locking it away in the shadows of my mind, which creeps out from its hiding place from time to time. Changing my mood in the blink of an eye, a distant memory a reminding fear, thinking how I really do not want to go visit there...
The heaviness hits hard like a rock, and I sigh, "What a crazy life I have led." Lessons learned, tears shed, pulling myself above all this dread.

How complex my very existence, trying to keep one step ahead of the game, trying to
Run out of the rain... The rain of thoughts that shadow over me, the past so hurtful,
Why did it have to be me? Picked from all the other souls waiting to be, picked to go
To this strange complicated family... What made me different from all the others? What lesson was I supposed to learn? Why me and not the others, why does my soul have to burn...

I try to run so far away, but the past catches up to me each and every day, so I turn to face my evil door; instead of running away, I go back for more… Now as the years have passed, I have come to finally see, all the lessons I have learned, and they do set me free… The hurt and pain will always be there, but now that I understand the truth, it's easier to bear.

I have made it through the rain… I now stand on the other side of the door… I dealt with all the pain and evil truths… They now lay out on the floor… What a strong person I am she, I made it through all my misery, and I know GOD has truly blessed me…

AND THE STORY CONTINUES......
SEASONS OF BEAUTY

One day I was walking down the hall with a co-worker. Our office was extremely busy with all the construction workers, trying to finish up all the details so we could move in. There was so much going on. People were coming and going all day long. We coexisted together for months.

Sharon and I were chatting together happily on this one particular day, and that is when I saw him. Here was this young man walking towards us with his boss. I had never noticed him before. I probably passed by him a million times, but on that day our eyes met for the first time as we came closer. He had dark hair feathered back (it was the 80s) and deep brown eyes, totally Italian. He smiled the most beautiful smile at me, and I smiled back. Our eyes danced and sparks flew, without us even speaking a word! I was totally smitten. As we passed each other, we both turned and looked back at each other smiling again. I turned to my coworker and said, "Wow, he was hot, and he had a nice ass too!"

"You have to appreciate a man in Levi's and work boots!"

We both chuckled and kept on going. Sharon turned to me and said, "He is totally your type I could see you hanging out with him." I just smiled.

After that day, I found myself day dreaming about this mystery man. I would walk the halls doing my job, and looking for him. I would stop and talk to people all the time as I made my way through the building. I became a total socialite enjoying everyone's company and always looking to make new plans so I would be out away from Mark and my mother! It was a great game plan for the time being. I was like a butterfly flickering from spot to spot taking in each and every moment. Taking time to smell the roses so to speak, learning how to live life.

Our Next Moment...

Then it happened again. I was at the desk of a co-worker going over something work related, and there he was. He was working right there in the closet. I looked up, and he was staring. He was staring very intensely. I could feel him. I smiled at him, but he just stared. It was awkward. I was not used to people staring at me like that, and it did make me feel uneasy, but totally excited at the same time. I had butterflies in my stomach. As I continued my conversation, my eyes kept on wandering up to him, as I was studying him. His deep dark eyes, his beautiful lips, and dark complexion, all I could hear in my head was WOW!!! I walked by him playing it cool and said hi! I was totally trembling inside with excitement. He didn't respond he just stared and smiled. I kept on going; thinking does he like me or is he just odd. Maybe he thinks I am weird??? So many thoughts ran through my head that day, and I was lost in thought. I kept going back to his lips, and wondered what it would be like to kiss him. Now the fantasies were rolling out in my head like a love song. My face was hot, my cheeks were red, and I had a permanent smile plastered on my face.

I went back to work, and tried not to think of him, as I was in such a mess already. I didn't need any more distractions, but I couldn't help it. It also didn't help that he passed down the hallway twice and walked right past my desk, pretending like he didn't see me, but I knew he did! I pushed through the rest of that day, but my excitement about him was over-whelming. Who was this dark sexy strange man, what was his name? What was he like? Now I am using the word sexy when thinking of him, and that is something that I have never done before. OK, I am in trouble!!

He would creep into my mind, when I was sitting on the couch watching TV with Mark, or when I was typing at my desk at work. I would see him every day now, but he wouldn't talk to me. At this point I figured he was shy. Then I would think maybe I am imagining the fact he might was interested in me. I did not want to look foolish. I would see him every day, smile and keep on walking. Most of the time he would smile back but would not speak a word. Maybe he had a girlfriend? I am totally confused!!!! So many emotions!!!!

Then one morning when I came into work I found my picture of me and my boyfriend on my desk turned down. This started happening every day! I thought now this is odd. Another day I went into my boss's office to find, his coworker at the desk working. He was a very bold young man, and right off the bat, said "Hi, how are you? I'm Denny." He was tall and slim with spiked up hair on top. He was half crammed under the desk fussing with the wires. He was a telephone man working with one of the companies installing the new equipment. I thought it was a little odd that he would want to strike up a conversation while twisted under that desk, but he did!

He was kneeling down, arms slumped on the desk and smiling, he wanted to talk!

I asked him what he was doing, and he was over excited to tell me. You can tell his personality was over the top and he was quite animated. Our conversation shifted and he made reference to his friend Johnny. I knew exactly whom he was talking about, and I was bubbling inside trying to down play my instant excitement of hearing him talk about my guy. Now I know his name, and that made him even more appealing. At this point my cousin comes in the office and joins the conversation.

Denny made a comment about Johnny always looking at me, and he played him up as a great guy. I was totally embarrassed, and my face went flush. My cousin chimed in and said the same thing. She was like, "I see him pass by her desk all the time, and he cannot stop staring!" They were laughing and teasing me, as I just stood there making a face. From that moment on, the three of us became friendly. We would talk all the time. Denny was hysterical, and he would always make us laugh. He was a lot of fun to be around, and made work not so stressful. We totally enjoyed his company, and looked forward to his antics every day.

One evening when my cousin and I were working late in the computer office, we hear voices coming down the hall and who popped in but Denny and John. Of course Denny was a chatterbox, coming right over, and asking a million questions. John stood silently for a while, and then he finally got up enough nerve to talk. He smiled and laughed as we all talked, and I fell in love right then and there. He had the most beautiful smile that I had ever seen, and his eyes were so intense he gave me goosebumps. I was definitely hooked. We talked about a lot of things that night, and realized we had so much in common, from our love of music and concerts, to horses and nature. At one point my cousin and Denny seemed to be nonexistent as we were so focused on each other. As we spoke their voices were so distant in the background, all I could think of was being with him. The chemistry was undeniable, and the energy was through the roof. I knew he felt the same way.

The one thing that we did not agree on was his beard. I hated it, and proceeded to tell him that he would look so much more handsome if he would lose the beard. He laughed at me and said never. We ended our conversation on a great note that evening, and it was Friday so my cousin and I were meeting co-workers for happy hour. We said our goodbyes and off we all went in our separate directions. That evening I confided in my cousin that I really liked him, and I didn't know what to do. She encouraged me to keep on talking to him, and give him a chance. She knew how I was feeling about Mark, and was just waiting for me to have the courage to end it. She agreed that he was totally into me, and we chatted about it over drinks like silly schoolgirls, it was a lot of fun. I didn't usually open up about my feelings so easily, but that night I sure did and it felt great.

Over that weekend, I could not stop thinking about John. I was at home and it was hectic, because my mom was acting up, but I didn't seem to care, my thoughts kept going back to him. I was with Mark, and my thoughts were back with John. I knew I was in love, and not with the man whom I was with. I could not hide these feelings for long. I kept on thinking about my commitment to Mark, and my duties and obligations. I was torturing my self. I was feeling angry, and distraught. I felt it was unfair that I felt such a deep sense of obligation to everyone but myself. Why was I like this? Why was I always putting everyone else first in my life? Why didn't I feel I deserved to be happy? I wanted to be loved more than anything in the world. All these thoughts rolled through my head all weekend long. I could not eat, and I could not sleep, I just kept on pondering these thoughts over and over again, it was maddening. I continuously put myself through the same roller coaster of feelings and emotions, but I could not seem to get beyond them. Why was I so stuck? What is it going to take to push me forward? I could not wait for Monday to come so I could go to work and see him.

Monday finally came. I am at my desk working, and he walked by. I could not believe my eyes. He was clean shaved. He took the beard off for me. He was so incredibly handsome. I was blown away. As he walked by, he smiled and pointed to his face, he was chuckling. I smiled and gave him a big thumbs up. I finished my work quickly, and found an excuse to take a walk. Of course, I found him. I told him how awesome he looked, and I was so happy that he did that. He said, "Lisa I did it for you. My mother thought I was doing it for her, and my girlfriend thought it was for her, but it was secretly for you!" Well, the ringing in my ears was so loud that his words sounded muffled. The butterflies were doing such a dance in my stomach; I thought I was going to pass out. I was flush once again. What was this man doing to me; he has taken my breath away. Yes, the only downfall—he had a girlfriend. At that moment, I didn't care. He was talking to me, and seemed to really like me. I felt so incredibly happy whenever I talked to him. It was like everything in my life didn't matter but him. He talked to me like I was the only person on the planet, so focused and intense. Our friendship bloomed from there. We talked every day.

I worked late most nights, and he would always come see me before he had to leave. He told me how he was not happy with his girlfriend, and just stayed because it was comfortable. He was not in love with her. That was music to my ears. I explained to him about Mark. I told him how I fell out of love with him, and I wanted out of the relationship, but I had obligations. John had a hard time understanding what that meant. Of course I didn't go into great detail about my life, as I did not want to scare him off. I told him a few things, but nothing heavy.

I looked forward to being at work even more now that we were friends. I had a lot of other men pursuing me at the same time, and of course I liked the attention, but my focus was on John. He was also well aware of my other suitors, and didn't like it. He made that crystal clear. He was jealous. He told me he really liked me, and none of the other guys were worth my time. I loved that; he was sweet and strong at the same time. He was honest, and that was truly comforting to me. He had strong work ethics, and a strong sense of family and loyalty.

He spoke very highly of his family, and was very much connected. Of course, that appealed to me. His parents were still together, and quite successful business people. He was the youngest of three, and spoiled rotten. What was most appealing was that even though he was spoiled, he was a hard worker and did not expect things to be handed to him. I respected that, and everything else about him. I think I fell in love with his family without even meeting them. He would tell me stories about all of them, and they sounded perfect! I would imagine what they looked like, and how it would be to spend time with them.

I started to share some of my family history with him, and when it came to my mother, I had a hard time telling him about her. I explained about her illness, and how she was crazy. I did tell him I was embarrassed of her, and it bothered me to feel that way. He seemed unfazed by it and said it's ok, don't worry about it. Our families and upbringings were polar opposites, and he just didn't care. That put me at ease, and it got a lot easier to talk to him. He was winning over my trust, and my comfort level with him grew.

As for Mark, we were at our worst. We could not even be in the same room without fighting. I told him, maybe we need a little break and he flipped out. He asked me if there was someone else, and I said NO. I didn't want to go there. I tried to explain to him how I was feeling about our relationship but he did not want to hear it, and told me that I needed to just stop it and we were meant to be together and that was it. I was so exasperated with him. After that conversation, I went silent. I would go visit, and just sit there like a zombie, waiting to leave. I was going through the motions. He was now starting to question me. He was suspicious, and kept saying he was going to track me down, if I was out without him. I was like, "I don't think so!" He was so jealous, and insecure he started acting like a crazy man. He would call me constantly, and accuse me of being out with men. I honestly wasn't. I was either working, or out with my co-workers or home. I would go walking with my dog or go to the gym, but he would never believe me. I was so done. He turned into this controlling monster!

I started telling John about what Mark was doing, and he told me that I should just break up with him, and get it over with. John didn't have patience for the waiting game, and he was like if its not working, end it and move forward. I knew he was right, but I was so scared. I just didn't know how to do it. I didn't know how to break free, but I wanted to so bad. The pressure I was under was unspeakable. I was riding the roller coaster of emotions 24/7, and I needed it to stop.

One Saturday in November I was leaving work, and John asked me if he could walk out with me. I said yes of course. We laughed and talked all the way to my car, which was parked right near his truck. We both turned on our vehicles, but continued to stand out in the freezing cold to talk. We did not want to leave each other. I had to go meet Mark that night, and he had a concert he was going to with his girlfriend. All the two of us wanted was to be together. We were so connected to each other. We stood there forever talking and freezing. We both knew we had to go, and that is when it happened. John leaned in grabbed me into his arms and kissed me. It was the most romantic kiss that I had ever had. I felt his love and passion through and through. He knocked my socks off. I didn't want it to end. I think I saw stars! We held each other for a long time hugging so tight, like we were never going to see each other again. When it was over, we just stared at each other and knew we had to go. I knew I loved this man with all my heart, and we had to be together. I had to find the strength to tell Mark. I didn't want to cheat on him; that would not be fair. John knew he had to tell his girlfriend as well. We said our goodbyes and we would talk on Monday. We got into our cars and drove in two different directions. I cried all the way home.

I made it through the rest of the weekend, and here we were back at Monday. I could not wait to get into the door. I arrived early like I usually did. I knew where John would start his day and went right there. He was there waiting for me, and we threw our arms around each other and just hugged for a long period of time. He eagerly shared with me that he told his girlfriend that he met some else and wanted to end the relationship. He was beaming ear to ear. He did it at the concert with all his friends around. It was a big mess, but he told her. He went on and on about how it happened, and everyone's reaction.

His friends were very clingy with him, and gave him a hard time about breaking up the crew, as they had all been friends through high school. John told them that he wanted to be with me, and I could be a part of it too. They basically said NO, and his friends were not kind, and were pushing him to make a choice them or me. John was shocked that they would do this to him. He thought they would be happy for him. He stated they were not in high school anymore, and he wanted to be with me! The reaction of his friends really surprised him, but he was a man on a mission and knew what he wanted. He saw the bigger picture. Then he looked to me, waiting to hear my story…

I told him that I didn't say anything to Mark. I got scared, but I decided I was going to; it was time. The smile drew away from his face instantly, he was annoyed with me, and the fact that I didn't do it over the weekend and pressed me to do it that day. He said to me, "You have to do it now!" I told him I couldn't but I would do it the next day. He was angry, very angry, but said, "Ok, whatever!" That day he was extremely cool towards me, and I could feel it. This is not what I wanted to happen at all. I felt even more pressure, as I did not want to loose this man. I promised him that I would do it as soon as possible.

The next day I met Mark on my lunch hour, and told him. It was pouring rain that day and we were sitting in his car in my driveway. Mark totally flipped out on me as soon as the words flowed from my lips! He first started screaming at me, than he cried like a baby. I was a little scared at first then I felt awful. All I could think about was I just wanted out of that car so bad, and run right into John's arms where it was safe. The rain was coming down in buckets and the echo of the rain pelting off the roof played an uneasy melody, as Mark sobbed out of control shaking. All I could do was just stare at him, motionless as the two sounds pounded through my head like a sledgehammer. It felt like an eternity before he spoke a word. When it was over, his last words to me were, "You cannot break up with me, and I wont allow you to. It is not over we are still together!" He repeated this like 5 times. I was like, "Are you kidding me?" Mark started screaming at me again, "You are my girlfriend, and I am not letting you go. I will be here tonight after work, we are going to stay together, you hear me!" His eyes were red from crying, but looked twisted and monstrous at the same time. I was shocked but I blurted out, "NO," but that didn't matter. He was not hearing me, so I got out of my car in the pouring rain, tripping through mud puddles stumbling to get to my car with my high heels on. I needed to get out of there, so I took off, and went back to work.

As I got out of my car, I was sopping wet, my hair was flat and my make up was running down my face, I was a hot mess. I could not believe he got so crazy. I ran directly into the bathroom to clean myself up, and headed back to my desk. My co-workers could tell something was seriously wrong with me, but nobody wanted to ask the questions! They just stared and went back to work. Mark started calling me at my desk, and screaming in the phone. I told him to stop, but he said he would only if I agreed to meet him that night. I said, "Yes," just to get him to stop. This was unbelievable. My head was spinning.

I just sat there for a moment to absorb it all. I was in even more of a mess. John was already not happy with me, and Mark was crazy. What do I do now? I just sat quietly, and proceeded to get some work done. When I had to get up and deliver some items to the other side of the building; that was my moment to go search for John. I knew where he would be working, and off I went.

As I walk towards him, he is making a disgusted face at me. I say can we talk for a moment? John, shrugs his shoulders and says, "Yeah, sure!" I told him what happened and he was mean to me. NO compassion at all!!! He told me I needed to stand my ground and just end it like he did. I tried to explain to him that it was not that simple, and my situation was complicated, but he was not sympathetic to my dilemma, and stood there with his arms crossed, mad as a hornet. John was tough, a typical Italian man, and he was holding me to my word! I told him I would talk to Mark again that night and make it crystal clear to him what my intentions were. John said in a snide voice, "Promises, promises." And put his head down and walked away. I just watched him, and my heart sank into my stomach, I felt sick.

Mark and I met up at my house, and proceed to pick up where we left off that afternoon, but this time we were inside. My family was sitting in the kitchen listening to every word, as we fought in the living room. I thought my mom was going to chime in a few times, as she was muttering random swear words, but surprisingly she did not intervene. So, I said my peace, and he said his. I was adamant that it was over and we did not have a future together, but my protest went upon deaf ears. He sat there and just glared at me for over an hour, than he just got up and left in silence. As he walked through the kitchen my mother blurted out "Asshole," and I heard the door slam shut. As he peeled out of the driveway, I knew that was not good, but I was so tired, letting him go was the best thing that I could do. He needed to cool off! I did not say anything to my family; I got up and took a shower, as I just wanted to go to bed. I did not want to talk any more.

As I came out of the bathroom, and was heading down the hall my mom started her bantering, and tried to throw her two cents in to aggravate me, but I totally ignored her, and decided to go sleep with my grandmother. I knocked on her door, and she said, "I was waiting for you." I went in and said, "How did you know I was coming in here?" Her reply, "Two words: your mother!" We both chuckled. I climbed into her bed and sighed. I needed someone to comfort me, and she was there for me whole-heartedly. She said, "Go to sleep Lisa, tomorrow is a new day, and everything will look clearer in the morning." She went on to say, "You need your strength to deal with this crap." As she was talking, I closed my eyes, and drifted off to sleep with her voice in the background. She was so strong and protective, I felt safe and warm in her bed that night.

I got up the next morning for work, and I felt like I never slept a wink. Crazy dreams filled my head, and I tossed and turned all night. When I walked outside Mark was in my driveway standing by my car. I rolled my eyes uttered a big sigh, and made my way over to him. He proceeded to taunting me immediately. I told him to leave I had to go to work. He told me he would be there when I got out. I told him go to work I do not want to see you. He was outraged and said he was going to chase me down every day, until I realized I belong with him. I was so sick to my stomach and angry that my rage got the best of me so I pushed him out of the way screaming, “Leave me alone!” and I got into my car and drove to work like a maniac.

My mind went directly to John and seeing him. I ran into work, and went directly to the place where he would be waiting for me. I told him the events of the evening, and what just happened. I was looking to him for support but he instantly gave up on me. He said that we were obviously not meant to be together, and I broke his heart. I was shocked!! I said, “How could you give up that easily?” He said, “Nothing ever comes to me that I really want anyways, so you not being mine just makes sense!” OK you say you want me, but you are willing to just walk away, because it is not easy? You must not want to be with me that badly then! I cannot believe you would just give up! Frustration was written all over my face as I was looking at him, trying to read his eyes. I was now extremely mad. He pondered for a few moments, looking away, and then he locked his eyes directly into mine.

With a stern look he said, “If you really wanted to be with me, then you would be with me. You are playing a game and I do not like it!” I said, “First of all this is not a game, I am a wreck, but I am working on it.”

His response to that was, “Come see me when you work it out.” He turned his back on me and walked away. I was devastated. I cried my eyes out all alone in that cubicle. The sadness that I felt was unbearable. Later that day, his friend Denny came to see me, and I explained it to him. He said John was working in the back warehouse all day angry and throwing things. He went on to say he would not talk about it, but he was definitely hurting, and had tears in his eyes. I told Denny I was working on it, and tell John it will happen, he needs to be patient. He needs to have faith in me. Denny said he would keep on talking to him because he knows we belong together, and this was all crazy business.

After that day, John would not talk to me at all. He did not even meet me in the morning anymore. We would pass each other in the hallway and he would ignore me, like I didn't even exist. This fueled me to take action. I knew I had to do something quick or I will miss out on an opportunity of a lifetime. I could not lose John, I was so deeply in love with him. I knew where I needed to be, and I was determined to make it happen. We finished out the week in silence John, Mark and I. I knew over the weekend I needed to fix it all and make it right.

I sat down with Mark, and told him everything I was feeling. I told him about John. I told him I just could not be in a relationship without love. I thanked him for being there for me, and I was grateful to have him in my world for as long as I did. He understood, but was very angry with me. He was hurt, and I understood that. He told me he loved me, and still wanted to spend the rest of his life with me. I destroyed his world, as he wanted to marry me. I felt sad. He went on to say that he wanted to still spend the holiday with me, even though I said we were done. He loved my dad, my sister, and the family. I stupidly enough agreed to it. As I still felt that obligation to him and the family. I thought maybe that would be the transition that he needed. I once again, was trying to help others before myself, and not putting my needs ahead of everyone else's. It seemed like I was always punishing myself for something I didn't do. Old patterns are hard to break.

I felt nothing was going to stop me from being with John. My mind was made up, I loved him and I was going to be with him. I knew Monday morning he would be mine, and I could not wait. I felt like Monday would be the beginning of a whole new world for me, and I was ready to jump in feet first. I so desperately needed this change, a new path to take that was exciting and fulfilling. The thought of it all was so intoxicating I could hardly eat or sleep. My mind was filled with so many fantasies of what was to come. I was walking on air.

Monday morning I was up bright and early eager to get to work. I walked in that door full of confidence and marched my way right up to John. I said to him we need to talk right now, and I was not taking no for an answer. I felt full of sass, as it was time to take control of my life, and get what I wanted for a change. My eyes sparkled with excitement as I could not wait to blurt out my personal victory.

I told him how I ended it with Mark for good, and I wanted to take a chance with him. I knew where I belonged and that was with him. I was beaming from ear to ear, and then the look on his face made me feel instantly unsettled. I said, "What is wrong? I thought you would be happy?" He just looked at me for a moment, and then said to me, "I went back to my girlfriend this weekend." Those words cut me like a knife. I was in disbelief. How could he do this to me! I yelled at him. I said, "How could you give up on me so quick, when you said how much you cared about me? What the hell is wrong with you!" He responded with, "I told you, you hurt me so I was not waiting." OHH, I quickly reminded him that he said come see him when I figured it out! I also told him, that I guess he didn't care that much because he couldn't even wait a week. I pointed my finger into his chest really hard and said "You are the game player, not me, asshole!" I was now steaming! So I pulled a John, I just turned around and walked away, the only difference here was my head was not down. I was muttering to myself all the way down the hall, quiet obscenities flying threw my brain. This was definitely not the dream I had in my head for what was going to transpire this morning. I was thrown into a tailspin. I went to work, and muddled through the day. I could barely speak or think. I avoided him all day. My world was crushed.

At the end of the day Denny came up to me, and I just cried. He said he knew John was in love with me, and did not understand why he would go back to the girlfriend that he could not stand. He said he was going to talk to John again, and he was going to get us together because he knew we were the real deal. At the same time, my cousin got a hold of John and read him the riot act for hurting me like that, and reminded him of how hard it was for me to do this, and I did it so I could be free to be with him. I showed him my commitment, and he just threw me to the sideline like trash. Now neither one of us was talking to him. John was dumbfounded by her words and remained silent.

The next few days at work were rough, but I fought through it. When I would get home, I would have to deal with the daily crap there with my mother. I was so over, hearing her repetitive words of shit! At this point it all meant nothing to me!

She would ramble on and on, cursing the world, and I was mute to her woes, as I could not even handle listening to it anymore.

I would run from the house every night, and just spend time with my dog. Champ was the best listener, and his unconditional love was exactly what I needed. My forever companion got me through a lot of bad times. We went to the beach enjoying the fresh air and freedom. I was able to relax, clear my mind and reflected on so many things. I felt lost. My life was flashing before my eyes. I was thinking about where it all started, and where I was now. I was also reflecting on how I transpired from a little girl lost to a grown woman lost. I was frustrated because the same old baggage was hanging on my back, and dragging me down, wrecking my future. I was thinking to myself when will all of this end?

My inability to put myself first for once, and allow myself to be happy, ruined my chances with someone that could be the best thing in the world for me. As I sat on the beach with my dog, I thought about how I never felt like I deserved anything good in my life. I was worthless. My family made me feel that way, Jerry made me feel that way, and now I was making myself feel that way. The skills that I learned on my own for coping with life sucked! I was now feeling anger towards everyone. I was feeling anger towards those who did not help me when I was hurting, and for my parents who never taught me good communication skills, or how to express myself at all. I was angry for being told repeatedly that I was nothing, and for the actions of others making me feel like I was not worth saving. I fought so hard to save myself for so long, that I never learned how to be happy once I got there. I decided that I was going to go after what I wanted. I was tired of not being truly happy. I was going to talk to John again, and he was going to be mine!

The next day I went into work, and I told him we needed to talk again. I laid it out on the line for him. I told him that my past had really messed me up, and I have a lot of work to do to help myself. It was a big part of why I had such a hard time letting Mark go. I told him that so many people took control of my life, and that made it easy for me to fall back into that pattern. I also told him that pattern breaks as of today. I professed my love that day saying "I am falling in love with you. I do not want to lose you before I even have a chance to be with you." I went on to say to him that he needed to tell his girlfriend he was done, and give us a chance we belong together. I was demanding that he be with me. I was not letting him go. I was adamant, and just stood there glaring into his eyes, like I was putting a spell on him.

John was shocked and a little taken aback by my assertive behavior, as he had never seen me act that way before. He told me that nobody had ever fought for him like that before, and he was amazed. He finally went on to explain himself more clearly so I would understand why he reacted to the situation the way that he did. He said he had low self-esteem, and was always giving up on things easily. If things got remotely hard for him, he always walked away. He was not proud of it, but this is who he was. I told him that was unacceptable, and he needed to fight for what he wanted. I also said, "In life if we do not go after what we want, we will never get anywhere, and never find true happiness!" He agreed with me, and said he would break up with his girlfriend that night and we would talk in the morning. So, I left it there and I walked away. I was hopeful that my honesty got through to him. I had to now wait it out. I felt proud of myself for being so assertive, and taking charge of the situation.

This was the new me, and I liked it a lot! It felt great, and no matter what the out come is, I spoke my peace and I was in full control of who I was as a woman in a positive manner. This was my new beginning of many wonderful things to come; I just didn't know it yet.

The next morning he came and found me, and this is how our conversation went…

"Good morning, Lisa! I looked up from my computer, and John was standing there. He flashed his killer smile at me, and I knew, but I played coy. In a very cold voice I said, "Good morning John, what are you doing here?"

"You know I am here to see you, and I thought we could we talk."

"I guess so," I say, and I continue to type on the computer. John stood there for a moment with this perplexed look on his face, and I went on to ignore him. He decided to come around the desk and placed his hand on mine. Chills ran through my body! "Please," he said. I looked up at him slowly, and my heart melted so I got up and he led me into the cubicle around the corner for privacy. I am just looking at him, trying not to show emotion.

"I want you to know that I broke up with my girlfriend last night."

"Oh, good for you," I say.

He responds, "Well I thought that you would be more excited than that?"

"Why?" I asked. "I am just as excited as you were when I told you that I broke it off with Mark."

"Come on Lisa, don't be like that, I came here for you." And he instantly pulled me towards him, and kissed me passionately. I melted into his arms, and felt fireworks going off around my head. Everything was light and airy, and I was dizzy. I suddenly snapped back into reality and I pulled back, and looked him in the eye and asked, "So, what does this mean?"

He said to me let me explain something to you. I saw you working here, way before you ever noticed me that day in the hallway. I watched you every day, even from the ceilings where I was working. I fantasized about you forever. I was the one who sat at your desk night after night turning your picture down, over and over again. I hated the fact that you had a boyfriend. The day our eyes met in that hallway, and you finally noticed me, I turned to my boss and said that is the girl I am going to marry! My boss said don't get caught up, there are a million of them in this building. I told him, no you are wrong, there is only one of her!

I was amazed at what I was hearing. I could not believe he watched me for so long. In my wildest dreams, I never thought a man would look and feel about me in such a loving way. So full of passion and conviction of his feelings, I was floored.

He went on to say that when I told him I could not be with him, until I got things straightened out with Mark, he was devastated because he waited so long to be with me, and felt it was all being taken from him. He reacted foolishly, and he was so sorry for hurting me. So again I asked him, "So what does all this mean?" He looked at me, and said "I am falling in love with you too! It means I want you to be my girlfriend, I want to take you out on a date and show the world you are mine. Will you go out with me, and be mine?"

"Yes John, I will," I responded and he kissed me again. Then we both simultaneously giggled.

He looked at me lovingly for a few moments, and said, "You are my poster girl, everybody wants you, but I have you!" I smiled and laughed, and then we kissed again.

On December 13, 1985, we had our official first date!

At this moment in my life I am not certain what is to come, but in this moment, this glorious moment I know I have found my soul mate. He completes me and I love him endlessly. In this moment of my life I am happy.

TOSTI

MasterCard
VISA
OPEN

SEASONS OF BEAUTY

Winds of change flow upon this delicate
Flower standing alone in a field of weeds
And thorns...

Covered by the old vines brown and
Stale looking to shine through the rubble
Of life...

This field of dreams out in the dark cold
Air, waiting for the sun to shine again.
This will stop the rain from falling
So hard, so long...

Winds changing, petals in the snow scattered
Like my broken heart torn to pieces, my
Heartache so deep...

This the day is upon us, when the sun shone
So bright, and this delicate flower finds its
Way through the field of pain, standing above
The rest...

My blossoming beauty so strong, bright and true,
Made it through the seasons, that real girl is you...

Epilogue

The Journey Continues

Epilogue

The Journey Continues

After that day so much happened in my life to bring me to this moment right here! I am now able to write my story. It has been a long and winding road with some serious twists, but I stand strong full of Faith and Hope that I will continue to move forward and grow with every new experience that is put in my path.

I have been through so much in my life. My upbringing was abnormal to say the least, and the abuse I endured was heinous. No child should ever have to endure such pain and loneliness the way I did. To be continually knocked down and isolated the way I was, it was truly damaging. I realize now looking back that as a teen I was going through PTSD (Post Traumatic Stress Disorder) and I didn't even know it, but how would I have known? Nobody ever came to me and said this is all wrong. What is happening to you is totally wrong! It needs to change today. I never got that. I never got the support I needed to realize that I was hurting as badly as I was. I looked good on the outside, but my insides were screaming for help even as an adult. At this point in my life, I am still affected by my past, and continue to cope with PTSD. I am still a work in progress.

Writing this book has been quite therapeutic for me, and validates what I was feeling and what happened to me. I know it was very wrong. I look at all my experiences as learning lessons, very hard lessons. I look back and know that I am at the head of the class. I have passed the test. I made it. I am a strong confident woman who has accomplished many successes along the way. I definitely have some major quirks, due to what I have been through, but I know I am not crazy. I am strong, determined, and willing to do what it takes to make things happen. The past has taught me to be tough and resilient. It has taught me that know matter how many times you're knocked down in life, you get up and fight harder, never let evil win.

I felt even as a young child, I had this deep inner spirituality that kept me going. I always felt something very different. I didn't always understand it, but I knew it was there. I also felt my brother was with me holding my hand along the way, guiding me through the worst of it, and telling me to hold on, it will get better. I had always hoped that one day it would be better, and I would live a good life, when all the torture and pain had ended. I would dream of it, I would hope for it, and I would pray every night that I went to bed that it would get better. I was determined to make it better. I fought with every inch of my being to find the goodness in my life.

Growing up with a mother who was mentally ill proved to be extremely difficult. I had to learn how to cope with things very differently from the average child. I lived in her manic world. As I grew older, and understood a little bit more about her illness, it helped me deal with her. As an adult she still puts a big damper on my life. It seems as if I am always running, and she is pulling me back into her mania. The countless phone calls and stunts that she has pulled along the way have been hard to deal with, even with the knowledge that I have today.

She is a constant stress in my life, and on my marriage. I love my mother dearly, and I wish it were different. I do not have a mom that

I can call and say let's talk! That would be dangerous. I cannot tell her anything that goes on, because she turns it around and makes it about her. It becomes a pity party for her. I always have to be careful about how I word anything. My children were robbed of a grandmother, like I was robbed of a mother. I feel that if my mother were treated differently as a child and young adult, she would not have hit such levels of mania.

At that time in our society, they frowned upon the mentally ill, and did not have the resources that they do today to help. It was a failure and an embarrassment to have a child who was sick. I feel bad for her, in regards to the fact that she could have been better than she was, but this seems to be her life path, and she travels it every day with strength and honor. She has accepted who she is, and what she is about. She still has a deep faith in God, and always remains hopeful. She says to me all the time, "Lisa, you know I am crazy, what do you expect?" I think about that a lot; what do I expect? After all these years, I still find myself wishing for a mom that I could go to. Wishing for a mom that would take care of me instead of the other way around. It is amazing that even as adults we yearn to have the loving touch of our mothers, and feel the safety of her embrace. I never had that, and I know I never will. I do accept that, but there are still those brief moments when I still yearn for it.

As for my father, he and I traveled an interesting road together. We had a special bond, and a deep understanding for one another. I still cannot believe he is gone, and I feel him with me every day. I miss him endlessly, as he always understood what I was feeling. At times I did not even have to say it out loud, and he already knew. Since his passing, I feel I am different. A part of me is gone, and I want it back. I yearn for my dad every day. Every day he does give me signs that he is with me, and that is comforting. I feel because my mom is so sick, that it why my dad's strength is what I drew from in times of need. He was always just a phone call away, and ready to listen and give advice. He was great for giving advice, as he felt he was a book of knowledge, and he was. His life experiences were tremendous, and he had a lot to offer. I feel I am a lot like him. My life experiences are incredible. I have been at the lowest of the lowest, and the highest of the highest. I road the roller coaster of life, and had the breath knocked out of me several times, but I kept on going. I now have the knowledge of many things, and wish to share them with you the readers, and anyone else who cares to listen. I feel my story, and experiences may help others, giving them a sense of hope when all hope seems to be gone. I feel it is my calling to share this with all of you, in hopes that it will help in some way.

My journey continues from here, and I want to write and share more of my life, so that others could benefit from it. I am a vessel of knowledge sailing across this big ocean of life looking to save others, as I have saved myself.

As I was on this personal quest to finish the book, my mother took a turn for the worst and got gravely ill. I took time off from writing, as I focused on helping her the best way that I could. Through the last few months of her life, she showed such great courage, and strength. She never lost her faith in God, or the hope that things would be ok. My mom always ran the show, her show! She gallantly made her way to the end of her life's path, with me by her side as always.

I supported her decisions, with much bantering from her family, but I knew what was best for her, and that was to let her die with dignity. These were her wishes, not mine, so I stood by her side and made sure all of her wishes were granted. Family came to say goodbye to her, and she had a really hard time in the last few days of her life. It was so hard to watch her suffer once again, as she had been through so much. I prayed for her to go peacefully, and sat with her playing music, and talking to her. In a brief moment of clarity she opened her eyes and looked directly at me and said, "Lisa, I am so sorry for what I put you through, you know how much I love you. When I am gone can I please come back and visit you?" I held her hand tight and I said to her, "Mom, I love you more than anything, and of course you can. I will be happily waiting for your signs." She closed her eyes, resting for a bit, and then started singing, "Bye Bye, Miss American Pie…this will be the day that I die…" It was eerie, but I knew it was her way of telling me that her time here was just about over.

My mother always feared that she would die alone or I would be alone with her when she died. She talked about this many times as it came closer to the end, but on the day of her death that was far from the case.

The nurses and doctors, along with hospice were so kind and loving to her. I came in that morning and she was sleeping. She was not talking anymore. I was sitting with her and my aunt randomly showed up. I was surprised to see her there. She stated that she had a funny feeling and she heard my mom say come now, and she did. We hung out for a while, and then the hospice nurse encouraged us to go get some coffee and stretch our legs for a bit. She assured us that my mom was not going anywhere just yet, and her vitals were still very strong. So reluctantly we went.

As we sat for a few moments talking, I had a funny feeling come over me, and I felt the chills. I looked at the clock it was 1:10 p.m., and I said let's go back upstairs I feel like something is happening. We went back upstairs and walked into her room, and I could tell she was dying. I went over to her and said, "Mom, it's ok to go. I love you." I put my hand on her chest, and her gift to me was feeling her last heart beat, and then there was nothing. I looked at my aunt and said I think she is gone! She told me to go get the nurse, and I did. They all came running down the hall, but I knew. I felt her leave. I saw a flash, and a glimpse of my dad and brother, as I turned to leave the room. The nurse confirmed she was gone, and my aunt turned to me and said, "Just like that! That's it!" I said, "YES!" We all just stood there for a moment taking it all in.

It was over, all the years of her pain and suffering was over. All the years of her abuse that she bestowed upon my aunt, so many others and me was over just like that, peaceful and calm. Mind blowing, is the only term I can use, to describe the moment. The years upon years of mania over in just one breathe. She was at peace.

At 1:17 p.m, she left this earth, with my father and brother by her side guiding her home, as she wanted. She spoke of them being there a few times in those last days, but she told them she was not ready, they needed to come back. That was so her, she had waited 43 years to hug my brother, but she told him to wait, why?

I know that answer, she did not want to be alone at the moment of her passing. She wanted her sister there with me, and she orchestrated it. When I had the feeling something was wrong, it was 1:10 (this was also my father's birthday), and the moment of her last breath 1:17 (March 17th, my brother's birthday). It all made perfect sense to me, it all had meaning as she wanted it to be. Nobody else but her!

She always said, "I choose life," but when she could not choose life anymore, she chose to die on her terms, with strength, pride and dignity. My mother did it HER way right until the end. There could be no other way; she demanded her final moment be about HER.

I love my mother with all my heart, and I miss her every day. I do not miss her mania, but I miss her the true Joann Sega, and I am proud to call her my mother.

She did tell me over and over, throughout the years, "Lisa, write a book about me and our life together. You will make millions!" She also told me that our family was very special and unique and there will never be another story like this one ever! I feel she had the wisdom to know the truth about many things. I believe she is correct—our story is quite unique and different.

When my dad passed away almost 5 years ago, it seemed that my spiritual gifts from my childhood started to resurface. When I was young and I would hear and see things, it terrified me. Every time it would come to the surface I would squash it out of pure fear. As I got older, like in my late teens and twenties, the dreams that I had intensified, and messages were given to me over and over again. I started to see and feel things. I always knew that was there, but I kept it at bay, but again after my father died things started to change.

I started to slowly embrace the fact that I had a gift, and it was special, but I did not really zone in on it. I just kind of left it there. After my mom's passing, many things for me have changed in regards to my abilities. My gift has intensified immensely. I am now embracing it and trying my best to understand it. I am not scared of it anymore. I am an extremely spiritual person, and I feel that is why it has come back to me. I can communicate with spirit, and I accept that now.

I am not sure where this will go from here, but I am open to new possibilities and I have a positive outlook on it. I feel I am a messenger reaching out to those in need. What I have been through in my life has opened me up to a whole new world of knowing. My mission is to help others, and hopefully bring comfort and peace to their lives. I have learned to always be humble, and to give back to others who need our helping hand along the way. This is who I am.

As I embark on a new phase in my life, I embrace it with open arms. I have many blessing in my life. I have my husband, my three children, and my two grandchildren, along with my extended family and friends that are all wonderful and caring people. I am so lucky to be surrounded by such an amazing group. My mother never wanted me to be alone, and I can assure her that I will never be.

My Life… Destiny or coincidence…

Maybe it was not a coincidence? Maybe it was the life path I chose before I came to this earth? This life, my personal journey, so that I could have this knowledge to share with all of you.

God Bless

Lisa

And my story goes on from here… to be continued….

Lisa

CPSIA information can be obtained
at www.ICGtesting.com
Printed in the USA
BVHW032004071121
621020BV00005B/244

9 781535 601481